LOWERING THE TONE

LOWERING THE TONE
& RAISING THE ROOF

RAYMOND GUBBAY

Quiller

To my grandchildren, Jessica, Ben, Emily, Jack, Joshua and Ella,

and please all find proper jobs and don't ever consider

following in Grandad's footsteps.

First published in the UK in 2021
by Quiller, an imprint of Quiller Publishing Ltd.

British Library Cataloguing-in-Publication Data
A catalogue record for this book is available from
the British Library.

ISBN 978-1-84689-352-0

Design by Guy Callaby

Printed in Great Britain by Bell and Bain Ltd, Glasgow

Quiller
An imprint of Quiller Publishing Ltd

Wykey House, Wykey,
Shrewsbury SY4 1JA
Tel: 01939 261616
Email: info@quillerbooks.com
Website: www.quillerpublishing.com

CONTENTS

ACKNOWLEDGEMENTS

The idea of writing a memoir was something that had been swirling around in my head for many years. Finally, it was my great friend and colleague Craig Hassall, CEO at the Royal Albert Hall, who encouraged me to write this and provided a deadline with the Hall's 150th Anniversary Year celebrations.

Johanna, the grandmother of my grandchildren, provided steadfast encouragement and read my evolving copy during a very pleasant stay in Malta. She also came up with the title for which I will be forever in her debt. My daughter, Emma, has worked tirelessly to locate ephemera, records and photos stored at her house in Ireland, helped enormously by Julie Pratt who prepared, photographed and scanned these images.

My grateful thanks also to Chris Christodoulou, Paul Sanders, Phil Dent and Clive Totman for their help with sourcing and selecting the photographs.

From an early stage, John Reiss and Simon Millward at Premier PR provided support and encouragement and suggested the most marvellous editor in Liz Marvin. Her wise counsel on what to include has been equalled only by her unvarnished views as to what to omit.

My publisher, Andrew Johnston, and his colleagues at Quiller Publishing have handled this project with relish and aplomb. I must also thank Neil Adleman and Amy Bradbury at Harbottle and Lewis and Louise Halliday and her colleagues at the Royal Albert Hall.

Finally, my many friends and colleagues for their curiosity, bemusement and support and their sharp memories in helping to rekindle events from sometimes long ago.

CHAPTER ONE

THREE QUESTIONS

'Where did you go to school?'
'Are you a Jewish boy?'
'Can you start on Monday?'

Three questions that changed my life.

I was well aware of the name of Victor Hochhauser; every weekend the newspapers carried his announcements for Sunday night concerts at the Royal Albert Hall and his seasons of Russian ballet and folk-dance companies. In one of those chance opportunities that seem to arrive just when they are most needed, my father had mentioned to Arnold Wesker, the playwright, that I was looking for a job in the entertainment business. The timing had been opportune because Wesker had soon afterwards met Hochhauser and mentioned that he knew a young lad who was looking for employment. It so happened that Hochhauser had such a vacancy and so I was summoned to meet the man himself.

The number 28 bus no longer starts from Golders Green but for all the time I lived there it did. Gliding out of the station depot, it cruised along the Finchley Road, turning off at West End Lane and eventually emerging at Notting Hill Gate before trundling down Kensington Church Street and on south. 'Look for the fridge shop on the corner of Church Street and Bedford Gardens,' I had been told. Once we got beyond Notting Hill Gate, I peered out, eager not to miss my stop. In between the antiques shops, jewellers and galleries was indeed, rather incongruously, a shop selling fridges. The office I was looking for was directly above this.

I mounted the stairs and emerged into a small general office with two girls busy at their typewriters. After a short wait — during which time the telephone barely stopping ringing — I was shown into a much larger room overlooking the street. A big man wearing a dark suit and heavy-framed glasses sat at a desk. The interview was brief, consisting of those three questions:

Where did you go to school? University College School, Hampstead.

Are you a Jewish boy? Yes.

Can you start on Monday? Yes.

There followed a supplementary question: 'How much do you expect to earn?' I pitched in at ten pounds a week, an advance of two pounds over what I had been earning at Pathé Newsreel, my last permanent job. He agreed immediately, suggesting that this was perhaps not to be my finest piece of negotiation.

I started working for Victor Hochhauser the following week. It was August 1964 and I was eighteen years old. And while I had not started out with any burning desire to be a concert promoter, I was nonetheless now very excited at the prospect of working for one of the best known names in the business. I had managed to dodge the family business of accountancy and I immediately felt that this was a field in which I would feel very much at home. I grabbed the opportunity with both hands.

I was allocated a space at the back of the outer office in a cubby hole alongside filing cabinets full of old programmes and paperwork of all kinds. Here were records going back over twenty years. All the correspondence with artists and their managers, the orchestras and, of course, the Russians. The constant ringing of the telephone was punctuated by Mr Hochhauser's voice booming out at every new call, 'Who's on the phone?' No sooner had someone tried to respond than another call would come in and the endless litany would continue. It was akin to undertaking a crash course in concert promoting.

My reading was augmented by daily practical lessons. 'Book a pianist for the Albert Hall Sunday concert!' was a command suddenly bellowed from the inner sanctum. On hearing these barked orders, Gillian, Mr Hochhauser's long-suffering secretary, would kindly guide me on. 'Ring Ibbs and Tillett,' (who were famous artists' agents) she said. They were still quoting fees in guineas (a guinea being the equivalent of £1.05). When I reported to Mr Hochhauser that I had found somebody on Ibbs' list and beaten their fee down from sixty to forty guineas, I was immediately instructed by Mr Hochhauser to 'offer them pounds'. It was a useful lesson: never accept the fee proposed and be creative with your negotiation. I had negotiated but the guineas-to-pounds discount was one I had not thought of.

It was not long after I had started work than I was made aware of my predecessor and allusions to his supposed 'misdemeanours', which were never fully explained. Robert Patterson was a few years older than I was. Before working for Mr Hochhauser, he had already done some work as an actor and also worked with the theatrical producer Harold Fielding. He had been entrusted with shepherding the Hochhausers' four children on visits abroad as well as being expected to look after ballet tours and concerts, and probably make the tea and coffee as well. He had recently left and had had the impudence to set up on his own — which, I guessed, was actually the full extent of his crimes. Not only that, but he had hired the Royal Albert Hall and was putting on a group called the Swingle Singers — an impressive booking.

A few days after learning of this fact, I noticed the stub of a five-shilling (25p) standing ticket for the Swingle Singers' concert in Mr Hochhauser's ashtray. As innocently as I could, I enquired, 'What are the Swingle Singers, Mr Hochhauser?'

'Rubbish,' he said. 'Rubbish put on by Patterson. If I offered a few pounds more I could get them but who wants it?'

Clearly the public did as the concert had sold out. Mr Hochhauser lost no opportunity in denigrating Patterson, as I often heard him doing during telephone conversations.

'I've got a young man working here, Raymond Gubbay. Would you take a booking from him?' he asked a venue manager one day whilst trying to impede Patterson's efforts to book a hall. But despite Mr Hochhauser's efforts, Robert Patterson went on to a major career, promoting international artists and tours and, in many ways, he blazed a trail for so many of the promoters who followed him and who work in the middle of the road and light entertainment fields.

I began working in Kensington Church Street when Victor Hochhauser was at the height of his powers. At forty-one, he had already broken new ground with a visit by the Kirov Ballet to the Royal Opera House. He maintained a virtual monopoly on bringing artists from the Soviet Union, had introduced David Oistrakh to the West, brought Richter for tours and had organised festivals for Russian artists and orchestras, none of which would have happened without the active involvement of his wife, Lillian, then three years his junior, although subsequent references to her in the press indicate that the age gap may have somehow later widened.

A glamorous mother of four young children, Lillian managed to look after the family, the business and Victor. She would smooth over his constant gaffes. While she would be talking softly on the telephone to rectify some slight caused by her husband, he would be calling out 'Who's on the phone, Lee?' (as he called her). Cupping the mouthpiece, she would tell him to be quiet but his persistence would eventually draw from her the caller's name. 'Tell him to go to hell, Lee. Tell him to go to hell.'

The cacophony was at times unremitting but it was great training – if you could work in this atmosphere, you could work anywhere. Also, it was very unpredictable; no two days were ever the same, which I really liked.

One day, quite early on, I found myself alone with Mr Hochhauser when the doorbell rang. 'Who's at the door?' he called out.

I went down the stairs to see, aware as I descended of being followed at a distance by the figure of Mr Hochhauser, his large frame blocking the light from the office above. I opened the door to find a gentleman dressed seemingly all in black but with a white shirt just visible under the gabardine. A homburg, a long beard and extensive side-whiskers completed the picture. He said something in Yiddish, which I do not understand, and Mr Hochhauser, now standing right behind me, ushered him in. An old friend come to call was my first thought, as nobody normally got beyond the threshold without an appointment.

After some minutes, Mr Hochhauser called through to me on the internal telephone, 'Can you make a cup of coffee for my friend?' Every few minutes some new request: did I have a map of London? How did one get to Leicester Square? Finally, he asked did I have a couple of pounds (a small fortune coming from Mr Hochhauser) in the petty cash for his friend? After the best part of an hour they emerged together from the office still talking animatedly in Yiddish. Mr Hochhauser showed him down the stairs, with me following, and let him out. As he closed the door, he turned to me and said, 'Raymond, you mustn't let people like that in here.' So not a friend after all! Clearly the man had been 'tipped the wink' by somebody in the know and had turned up on the basis of assuming that Mr Hochhauser would not send him away empty handed; he was absolutely right.

Occasionally, as I lived near the Hochhausers, I would get a lift from one of them. One morning I had arranged to meet Mr Hochhauser at his house so that we could drive to a meeting. He had a lovely Jaguar and a penchant for reversing out of his drive in the full expectation that everything passing on the Finchley Road would stop for him. On this occasion, as he started to back out, two double-decker busses were bearing down on him from both directions, tooting their horns like crazy and forcing him to pull up very sharply. 'Anti-Semitic swine,' was his only comment.

In the office one day, I overheard Mr Hochhauser talking very loudly on the telephone to Mstislav Rostropovich. It appeared that the great cellist was about to elope with the Countess of Harewood, the former concert pianist Marion Stein. Mr Hochhauser was warning Slava, as Rostropovich was known, that he would have nothing more to do with him if he went ahead with his plan. The story never went any further but the consequences had it have done so would have been profound. This was the 1960s and, although the decade was subsequently dubbed the Swinging Sixties, polite society wasn't yet ready for such behaviour from the wife of the Queen's cousin. In the end though, the Harewoods did divorce three years later and Marion Stein married the Liberal politician Jeremy Thorpe in 1973. I even saw them together many years later at one of the recitals I promoted for Ivo Pogorelich at the Barbican.

After just a few weeks in the office, I undertook my first touring assignment working with the Moiseyev Dance Company who were performing a three-week season at the Royal Albert Hall immediately after the conclusions of the BBC Proms season, followed by a regional tour. The company included, at the time, the granddaughter of Anastas Mikoyan, the Soviet Foreign Secretary who had joined with Lenin at the time of the 1917 revolution. This created a lot of newspaper interest and even a press story drawing parallels with Winston Churchill and his actress daughter, Sarah.

To all intents and purposes, I was Mr Hochhauser's quasi-representative on the spot. Looking back, I find it hard to imagine how he could have placed quite so much trust in me. True, I was cheap labour and he was never that far away in case of urgency but, at the same time, this was the era of telephone boxes and letters in the post; both mobile phones and email were decades in the future. Being young, I was not at all daunted by the weight of my responsibilities, and I was lucky. The company spoke little, if any, English but the interpreters working for Mr Hochhauser were very experienced and could be relied upon for sensible, helpful advice. Nonetheless, it was extraordinary, marshalling three coach loads of Russians round the country, making sure they knew when to be ready, getting the luggage properly labelled so it ended up at the right hotel (if we were spread over more than one, as did happen sometimes), liaising with the theatres in advance so they knew what set-up was required and so on. On a few occasions, I even went to the bank with one of the Russians and cashed a cheque for £4,000 which we carried off in a shoe box – that was quite an experience as I had never seen that much money in my life. It was a whole new world which I loved; I could never imagine going back to work with a nine-to-five job in an office.

The year 1964 was the height of Beatlemania and Moiseyev was persuaded by Mr Hochhauser to dress four of the male dancers in Beatles outfits for one of the numbers. I was sent to Carnaby Street, then the street to visit for outré clothing, to find suitable attire including wigs. Fortunately, common sense in the shape of Igor Moiseyev's theatrical nous took over and the idea was dropped, but not until after quite a lot of press publicity had been generated.

On the first night at the Albert Hall, I had to take a chair onstage and move a microphone at the start of a number for one of the musicians. He was accompanying the performer in *The Fight of the Two Urchins*, a comedy number where just one character with his back arched and moving nimbly on hands and feet portrays two boys fighting each other. The special costume he wore completed the illusion. I got a big round of applause but managed to delegate the task elsewhere once Mr Hochhauser announced that I would have to don a folk costume for every subsequent performance.

Once the season got under way, the daily routine of performances became very enjoyable and I liked working at the Royal Albert Hall. Somewhere in the bowels of the hall near the backstage area were the boilers and it was quite normal to see through an open door the stoker, legs stretched out in front of him, having a snooze whilst the fire from the open boiler door warmed the room.

The Royal Albert Hall at the time was lost in a time warp. The traditions which had been established when the hall opened in 1871 were very largely still in place. The Honorary Corps of Stewards with their silver badges, sometimes handed down from father to son, were in charge of the public areas. Backstage was cramped with barely enough space for a big company like the Moiseyev. The wigs were 'dressed' in the corridor, costume rails were shoved into any available space and the dressing room accommodation, such as it was, was very cramped. Front-of-house facilities were not that much better with inadequate bars and, at that time, no permanent restaurant. The staff though were wonderful, very helpful and with seemingly endless patience for a young tyro like me. The company too was fun when they could relax but all too often one felt the dead hand of the commissars and their acolytes controlling the reactions and emotions of the entire company. One funny moment was when one of the dancers asked me if I could get him some 'preservatives'. Innocent as I was, it took some considerable time and a bit of graphic miming to make me realise that he was not after all talking about jars of strawberry jam. The staff at the artists' entrance became my friends and Tom, who manned the switchboard in a cubby hole near Door Six (the main entrance on Kensington Gore), was a lively soul. 'How are you today?' I'd ask as I passed by. 'Up and down like a bride's nightie,' was the usual response.

Then one day, quite suddenly in the middle of the season, there was a panic. In Moscow, Nikita Khrushchev, First Secretary of the Communist Party and therefore head of state, had been deposed in a putsch and it looked as though the company might have to return home immediately. The atmosphere backstage became tense but after a couple of days the crisis passed. 'I see Khrushchev's been kicked out,' I said, not very diplomatically, to one of the more senior artists who had a smattering of English. 'Khrushchev old, Khrushchev sleep,' was the enigmatic response. I do not think Khrushchev would have seen it quite that way as he was forced into retirement.

When the Albert Hall season finished, I found myself out on tour almost on my own with over one hundred Russians. The first regional date was the Brighton Hippodrome on what turned out to be the last show at the theatre and we moved around the remains of the old Moss Empire theatre circuit for the next few weeks. This was a time of decline for regional theatres and the Moss Empire circuit was but a shadow of its former self. In its heyday, between about the 1930s and 1950s, this great chain of theatres — which included the London Palladium and the Hippodrome in Leicester Square — had been hugely influential and the biggest touring circuit in the country, providing regular work for many performers. The rise of television coinciding with the decline of the music halls and variety houses had had a major effect on its business.

When we arrived in Manchester, I received a call from Mr Hochhauser. He told me he needed me to send a telegram in his name from Manchester, as he wanted to get out of going to a wedding. 'Write this down,' he ordered. The opening word was 'mazeltov'. Pretending ignorance, I asked him to repeat it not once but twice. I heard him scream out to his wife, 'Lee, Lee, he's a Jewish boy and he doesn't even know how to spell mazeltov.'

During the tour, the company returned briefly to London to appear in the Royal Variety Show at the London Palladium. It was an exciting experience for me to see so many well-known faces all together. I sat in the stalls during rehearsals listening to Robert Nesbitt, who always directed the show, being rude to Lena Horne because she would not follow his advice about what she should be singing. Tommy Cooper was very funny and Gracie Fields sang a number of her best known songs.

The tour staggered on but the audiences were not that great. Earlier tours of the Red Army and various folk ensembles had been very popular but the trouble with Moiseyev's company was that it was a little too classy. Moiseyev was a great choreographer — after all, he had been the original choreographer of Khachaturian's *Spartacus* many years previously for a production at the Bolshoi. He had a knack of being able to take folk melodies and forge them into interesting choreographic dances. In his work, there was even an occasional harking back to an earlier, pre-Revolutionary age, almost as if a curtain would suddenly be drawn aside quite unexpectedly on a small slice of Russian provincial life as it might once have been. As a Jew who had to both carefully and loyally follow the official Soviet line, it was his neck that was quite literally on the line should anyone try to defect. The gopak which ended the show was an endless kaleidoscope of acrobatic twirls and leaps ending with one of the soloists launching himself to jump, legs akimbo, above the whole company. However, to my mind the best of all was *Partisans*, recalling the brave bands of Russian fighters who harried the invading Germans in the Second World War. The opening sequence of seemingly mounted riders weaving and circling the stage still remains in my memory to this day.

Although artists and ensembles from the Soviet Union were always warmly welcomed by British audiences, the strong feelings of friendship and common alliance made during the Second World War had come to an end. The Berlin Airlift of 1948, when the 'Reds', as the Russians were commonly called, tried unsuccessfully to force the Allied forces of Britain, France and the USA to abandon Berlin, had put an end to any semblance of unity between the Soviet Union and the other victorious Allied powers.

The Soviets tried very hard to persuade their citizens that life in the West, as portrayed to them, was just a front. When the Bolshoi Ballet came to London in 1956, they had been told that the shops had all been specially altered for their drive down Oxford Street and that the goods on display were not normally there. Of course, nobody in the company, probably not even the most diehard member of the Communist Party, believed this but they had to pretend that they did. This perpetual state of unreality always had to be maintained, not least because nobody ever quite knew who was informing on whom. The system relied on a web of informers at every level.

It did not take me long to work out that the company was riddled with a hierarchy of apparatchiks who had to report on their fellow performers. There was also a beefy looking young man who appeared to have no official function.

'What does Boris do?' I asked the interpreter one day, in an innocent-sounding voice.

'He's here to look at the stages,' she replied.

He was, as I discovered, rather more than that; it was he who actually controlled the network of informers, using them to keep abreast of any potential problems. On tour, it was he who decided who could share rooms and even who had to accompany whom for shopping trips. Everything was totally controlled by him as it was his neck that was quite literally on the line should anyone try to defect.

In Bristol, we had a visit from Rudolph Nureyev, who had himself defected three years earlier. Margot Fonteyn's secretary accompanied him and I was asked by Mr Hochhauser to look after them. I greeted them front of house before the Saturday matinee, saw them seated and arranged interval refreshments. At the end of the performance, Nureyev insisted on going backstage. When the company members saw him, they all pointedly turned their backs on him, even when he tried talking directly to some of the dancers. There were even hisses and some seemingly mild but probably to him quite offensive barracking. He left shortly afterwards through the stage door, dejected and sorrowful at having been unable to talk to anybody. I felt afterwards that some of the performers would really have loved the opportunity to engage with him in conversation but they were simply too afraid to do so.

Our last date on the tour was Liverpool. We travelled the short distance from Manchester on the Sunday and were due to open at the Empire Theatre the following day. On the Sunday itself, the Beatles were playing two concerts at the theatre and Mr Moiseyev asked me to arrange for him to see the show. There were of course no seats available so I found myself standing at the back of the stalls with him and his wife waiting for the Fab Four to appear. The compere worked the audience up to a frenzy, spelling out each name in turn and encouraging ever louder roars each time. It was almost impossible to hear the Beatles perform at all such were the unending screams and roars from the audience. Just before the end of the second performance, I went backstage to watch the last few minutes from the wings. As the curtain came down on the final number, the four rushed offstage and out of the stage door into a waiting car. Before the audience even had a chance to realise that they were not coming back on stage, they were long gone. After that performance, our opening the following evening seemed to lack a certain something.

At the end of the tour, which had not been a great financial success, the Hochhausers arranged a farewell dinner for the company. There was a lot of false bonhomie over a very mediocre meal, at the end of which Mr Hochhauser stood up to make a speech. 'My dear friends,' he began, 'all good things must come to an end and the time has come for us to part,' and so on in a similar vein. He concluded by saying, 'So let's hope that in two or three years' time, you'll be back for another tour.' The next day, I drove back with him from the airport after we had seen them off on their way home. 'Two years,' he said. 'I hope they don't come back in twenty years.'

With the tour over, I found myself once more back in the office amidst the usual cacophony of calls, shouts and mild expletives. Besides the tours and seasons which he arranged, Victor Hochhauser was well-known for his Sunday night concerts at the Royal Albert Hall. These were often the music of Tchaikovsky or Strauss, popular concertos or concerts that would reliably draw audiences into the hall on a Sunday evening. From the late 1940s, he had a virtual monopoly on these and they continued to flourish, albeit on a diminishing scale, until after the Barbican opening in 1982. Allowing for the BBC Promenade Concerts and certain other regular events, he probably had about thirty Sunday nights a year. I had to attend many of these, including one at which Sir Malcolm Sargent was conducting the Royal Philharmonic Orchestra.

It was early in the New Year in 1965. Winston Churchill was seriously ill and there was grave concern that he might not pull through. After every movement of the *New World Symphony*, which made up the second half of the concert, Sargent put down his baton and came offstage. He wanted to know if there was any news. He had even asked the orchestral librarian, George Brownfoot, to include in each musician's folder of music the slow movement of Beethoven's *Eroica Symphony*, often played at funerals, just in case, as he was clearly determined to be the first with a tribute. In the event, Churchill survived for a couple more weeks and the concert ended without any changes.

I quickly became accustomed to spending my Sundays at the Royal Albert Hall. One day I sat next to Mr Hochhauser during an afternoon performance by Tony Praxmeyer's *Gay Tyrolese from Kitzbuhl*, not a natural title nowadays for family entertainment. This happy group of thigh-slapping, smiling Tyrolians in traditional lederhosen entertained a capacity audience with an Austrian knees-up. Mr Hochhauser was smiling broadly, 'Rubbish, isn't it? But they love it,' he said, indicating the audience.

I stayed on for the evening concert, not promoted by Mr Hochhauser, but the very first London appearance of the New Philharmonia Orchestra after they had reformed themselves into a self-governing organisation following Walter Legge's decision to disband the old Philharmonia Orchestra. Again, it was a capacity audience, a completely full house, only the music was rather more sublime – Verdi's great *Requiem*, conducted by Carlo Maria Giulini, who had wanted to show his support for the new orchestra. For the ride home on the 28 bus I was almost floating on air.

The next tour was due to take place in the spring. 'The Red Navy Choir' was actually one of several ensembles attached to various naval stations around the Soviet Union. The name had been invented for the purposes of this tour in a clever move by Victor Hochhauser to follow on from the enormous success enjoyed in Britain by the Red Army Choir, which had captured the public's imagination as representative of our great wartime ally rather than the acceptable face of a repressive Cold War regime only just recovering from the excesses of Uncle Joe Stalin's purges. This group was based in the Crimea and was notionally part of the Black Sea Fleet. However, I think the attachment must have been rather tenuous as the all-singing, all-dancing group looked as though it had hardly ever been to sea.

We opened the ten-week tour at the Bristol Hippodrome. Each programme started with the two national anthems, ours emerging in guttural Russian tones as 'God save their gracious Queen', and included the obligatory rendering in broken English of 'It's a Long Way to Tipperary' amongst the usual mixture of fast and furious folk dances, sailors' dances and Russian folk songs with the odd semi-propaganda number slipped in. The more obvious numbers extolling life in the Soviet Union such as 'Down on the Collective Farm' tended to be excised from foreign tours.

For the opening performance, I had been asked by Mr Hochhauser to arrange for a big basket of fruit to be presented on stage at the end of the performance in full view of the audience. I suppose he thought it was more appropriate than flowers. So I had a beautiful presentation basket prepared by a local store – brightly polished red apples, large oranges, pineapples, grapefruit, a whole array of lovely looking fruit, each piece perfectly positioned. I went onstage to present the basket as arranged. After the final curtain, Mr Hochhauser asked me to retrieve the basket and to present it at

....

every subsequent performance. I assumed he meant just for the week at Bristol but he told me that I had to take it on the entire tour.

The next week, not surprisingly, not all of the fruit was at its best and I asked if I could replace some of the more pallid looking pieces. I was told to please do the best I could rather than buy any more fruit. So for the next nine weeks I found myself adjusting and moving the fruit around, trying to find an unbruised surface of an apple and a side to a pineapple not showing signs of rot. Anyone attending a performance at the end of the tour might have been surprised to observe me come on at the final curtain carrying at arm's length a basket of fruit and placing it on stage in front of the company. By this time, none of them wanted to touch it. It was just as well that it was not mid-summer otherwise it would probably have been accompanied by a cloud of fruit flies!

We travelled between venues in three coaches every Sunday. The tour was not terribly well planned and often involved long journeys across country. We would stop off for a comfort break mid-morning and I would sometimes take the opportunity to report in to Mr Hochhauser. I would call him at his home from one of the new telephones which allowed one to dial direct to almost anywhere in the country. Prior to this, anything other than local calls had to go via the operator. The minimum acceptable coin was a threepenny bit (just over one pence) which was inserted once the call had been answered. I could not resist on one occasion when we were near the start of our journey, which I knew would take over ten hours, ringing Mr Hochhauser and, when the familiar voice answered, putting in the coin and pretending I could not hear him. To make matters worse, I kept muttering that I had something terribly important to tell him and that the phone system was rotten. The pips sounded indicating the last ten seconds of the call. I remember the ever increasing crescendo at the other end: 'Raymond, I can hear you, I can hear you!' before the phone cut off.

At the end of the day, we arrived at our hotel where an urgent message was waiting for me to call Mr Hochhauser immediately. After a leisurely bath and a meal, I called him.

'Raymond, I'm so worried, what's happened?'

'What do you mean?' I replied.

'You called me; I could hear you.'

'Oh that,' I said. 'It's OK, I sorted it.'

In the middle of the tour we reached Coventry. On Monday morning, as had been arranged at each new town, the company paraded in their smart Russian naval dress uniform for the march to the war memorial to lay a wreath. As usual, the local dignitaries turned out including, on this occasion, the mayor, the town clerk and the local police superintendent. A good photo opportunity was created which usually guaranteed a helpful spread in the local papers. It went well and we settled down to a week at the Coventry Theatre.

On the Wednesday afternoon, I was resting in the hotel when I received a call from the police station to say that they had arrested one of the Russians and he was being held in the cells, accused of shoplifting. Some years earlier, there had been a major diplomatic incident when a Russian athlete had been caught shoplifting in Oxford Street. Mindful of this, I called Mr Hochhauser — 'Bail him out, Raymond, bail him out!' was his only response. So I rushed down with our interpreter to the police station where an extremely worried-looking Russian sailor denied he had taken a pair of cufflinks from Woolworths, which just happened to have his initial on them, a B, the equivalent of the Russian V, for Volodia. The chief superintendent had been summoned — two days earlier he had been marching with us, now he was here to sort out a potentially explosive diplomatic situation. In the end, the police let the sailor go without pressing charges.

At the theatre that night, after the performance, the company held a meeting at which he recounted his experience. Captain Chikachev, the KGB agent in a naval uniform who had, I discovered, only joined the group at Moscow Airport, warned them to be on their guard against British agents provocateurs, especially in Woolworths. For the unfortunate sailor involved, I am sure worse was to follow because he would almost certainly never have been allowed to go on tour again — a severe punishment at a time when very few Russians were able to travel abroad at all.

In Manchester, we had a visit from the Russian naval attaché based at the embassy in London. These tours were a marvellous opportunity for embassy personnel to be able to apply for permission to travel beyond the normal limit of fifty miles from London. Local special branch officers, who made no attempt at discreet surveillance, followed him quite openly for his entire visit.

When he walked from the hotel into central Manchester, a kerb-crawling unmarked car tailed him with the plain-clothed officers inside. Mind you, I am sure they had good reason. In Bristol during the Moiseyev tour, an embassy official had asked me if I knew how far it was to the British Aerospace factory at Fairford in Gloucestershire. The naval attaché later asked me why we were not touring to Scotland — presumably he would have liked an excuse to get near to the new Polaris base under construction at Faslane!

In Birmingham, Mr Hochhauser invited half a dozen of the senior members of the company to lunch. Faced with menus in incomprehensible English, they did then what they always did and asked the host for his recommendation. I saw Mr Hochhauser scanning the menu and spying something at one pound, two shillings and sixpence (£1.12). 'This,' he announced, 'is the house speciality.' Then he noticed just below another main course at just one pound, one shilling (£1.05). 'Ah, but this,' he said, 'is even better.' They ordered it to a man.

At the end of the tour, there was another farewell dinner. I had been instructed to ensure that the beer was poured into each glass in order to get two glasses from each half pint bottle. Towards the end of the dinner, Mr Hochhauser got up to make a speech. 'All good things must come to an end, my friends,' he announced, 'and the time has come for us to part ... '

For the summer of 1965, Victor Hochhauser had announced a visit by the Bolshoi Ballet to the Royal Festival Hall. Back in the office at the end of the Red Navy Choir's tour, I found myself sidelined into dealing with the rather less interesting arrangements for the visit. A more experienced company and production manager was employed, which was probably just as well given my lack of experience, but I did not quite see it like that at the time. After one particularly stormy day, which started with Mr Hochhauser waking my mother on the telephone at an early hour and screaming at her to find me, I decided to give in my notice. I had worked there for ten months, twenty-eight days and twelve hours. At nineteen, I was once more unemployed.

CHAPTER TWO

GOLDERS GREEN

I was born in London in 1946 but that is almost the only British link of which I can boast. Well, my mother was also born in London in 1910 but, again, with not a drop of British blood in her veins. Her father came from a long line of Lutheran peasant farmers originating in Lithuania but who had settled for at least 300 years in East Prussia, then part of the German Empire (but since the end of the Second World War, Russian territory, the Kaliningrad Oblast). My great-grandfather fought on the Prussian side in the Franco–Prussian War of 1870, losing a leg at the Battle of Metz.

My maternal grandfather was a furrier who came to London to set up in business. He met and married my Jewish grandmother who had knocked ten years off her age so that she appeared five years younger than him. As far as I know, she kept up the pretence all her married life. She had arrived in England with her parents and ten siblings in the early 1890s from Latvia, forced out by the Tsarist pogroms. My grandfather never applied for British nationality and was interned during the First World War on the Isle of Man as an enemy alien before being repatriated to Germany in 1918. My mother, together with my aunt and my grandmother, followed at the end of the war in 1919, taking eight days to reach Berlin via the Hook of Holland and sustained largely by handouts from the Red Cross.

My grandfather re-established himself in Berlin as a furrier but was eventually allowed to return to England in 1930. My mother had lived in Berlin right through the period of the Weimar Republic and the period of hyperinflation. People would pay for their coffee as soon as they had ordered it and my mother used to recall how once when she went to get wool for her mother, she did not have the right money and went home to collect more. By the time she had returned, the price had already increased.

Even as a child, my mother was an excellent pianist. Both her mother and one of her aunts had taught music and so it was only natural that she would go on to teach music in Berlin, where her pupils included the three children of the hotel proprietor where she stayed as part of this arrangement. She was extremely happy teaching music in Berlin and imagined that she would stay there after her father had been allowed back to England. The following year, she returned to London for her parents' silver wedding anniversary but her father insisted that she remain. He could see the menacing dark clouds of Nazi Germany growing alarmingly. A few months later he died, aged only fifty-nine, stricken by a combination of grief over what was happening to his homeland and, as my mother was wont to say, rather a surfeit of brandy. Sadly I never knew him but I rather think I would have liked him very much.

The only surviving sibling of my grandmother's was her sister Helena who had been a singer of some distinction. Her greatest claim to fame, however, was that she was a friend of a fellow artiste (as they were then called) who went under the professional name of Belle Elmore. She was Corinne, the wife of the notorious Dr Crippen. In 1910, he murdered her, buried her body under the floorboards and fled with his young lover, Ethel Le Neve. They boarded the *SS Montrose* bound for Canada, she disguised in boy's clothing, masquerading as his son. However, the ship's captain became suspicious and had telegraphed Scotland Yard to say he thought that Dr Crippen had boarded the vessel under an assumed name. So a Scotland Yard detective was dispatched on a faster vessel which reached Quebec ahead of the *Montrose*. As the ship arrived, the inspector went out on the pilot's launch and was thus able to arrest Crippen as the boat docked. This was the very first occasion when the Marconi telegraph had been used to apprehend a criminal. Crippen was brought back to England, found guilty of murder at the Old Bailey and subsequently hanged.

My aunt remembered very clearly going several times to the Crippen house in Hilldrop Crescent in Holloway, which was close to where she lived. She and Belle Elmore had both appeared on various occasions on the same concert bill but at which venues I sadly do not know. During the First World War, she sang at concerts for the troops and after she died in the mid-1960s my mother brought home some of her old sheet music.

Music from that period was still played and so was familiar to my brother and me. On one occasion, on the return from a drive and lunch in the country, we were for whatever reason belting out the old wartime favourite 'Mademoiselle from Armentieres, Parlez-vous?' My mother suddenly came out with the line, up until then quite unknown to my brother and me: 'Up the stairs the sergeant went, when he came down, cor, his knees were bent.' My dad nearly had a fit and stopped her continuing. We, of course, being small boys, thought it was all very funny and, inevitably, such incidents stick in one's mind.

Nor did I know my paternal grandfather who had also died long before I was born. He was brought up in Aleppo, then within the Ottoman Empire, now in modern-day Syria, amongst the thriving community of Jewish merchants based in the city. His father, my great-grandfather, had been born in Baghdad where I believe the family had lived for a great many years. My dad always harboured the romantic notion of our ancestors being forced out of Spain by Ferdinand and Isabella at the time of the expulsion of the Jews in 1492 but the truth I fear is rather more mundane. Many of the Sephardic Jewish exiles from Iberia moved across to the Middle East and their rituals were adopted by the indigenous community. So everything points to my dad's ancestors coming from amongst the Mizrachi Jews of Iraq and Iran. They might even have been around in Jerusalem when Nebuchadnezzar destroyed Solomon's temple. Now that is an even more interesting twist to the family history than Ferdinand and Isabella!

The changes in India following the uprising in 1856 and the transfer of power to the British Crown from the East India Company opened up new trading opportunities for the Jewish merchants of Baghdad and Aleppo. My grandfather eventually followed, setting up in business as a broker in jute and gunny (used for making sacks and bags) in Calcutta, where my father was born in 1912. My grandfather's business failed in the late 1920s and he died soon afterwards. My grandmother, with great enterprise and not much money, booked passage for my father, then aged eighteen, his sister, two years younger, and herself to Venice and then overland to England to join relatives living in Edgware at the end of the Northern Line. My father completed his articles and qualified as an accountant, soon setting himself up in sole practice in Holborn. He first met my mother in the late 1930s at a dinner party but they only started courting (that wonderful expression of the time) in 1940 after the start of the war. They married in March 1942 and my elder brother was born exactly nine months later.

There was always music in the house for as far back as I can remember. My mother played the piano to a very high standard. She had studied with a pupil of the great Schnabel and in different times might well have gone on to a professional career. The war and marriage put an end to any such plans. My father played the violin and he and my mother were forever playing chamber music together or with friends who joined them to form a larger ensemble. Being a typical little boy, I found it all rather boring and probably lost no opportunity to say so. Even so, as I played with my toys and my friends, I guess not all the music was washing over me; some of it was starting to stick. Although I have the shame of knowing that I failed the RAM Grade One piano exam when I was seven, I nonetheless seemed to absorb music, even if I tried to keep it under wraps. Something of my parents' love and enthusiasm for music certainly rubbed off on me. I cannot hear Beethoven's piano sonatas or Chopin's waltzes, nocturnes and preludes without moving back in time to our house in Rodborough Road, to the sights and smells of the 1940s and 50s. To a world of rationing and utility goods, a world dominated by radio with no television, car, fridge or washing machine.

My mum's piano playing took her to many different places, though often small-scale concerts at old people's homes. One visit was very different. My cousin Mickey had a lovely mezzo-soprano voice and my mother sometimes accompanied her. In 1956 they found themselves giving a recital to prisoners at Holloway jail a few days after Ruth Ellis had been hanged. The case had caused great public debate. Ruth Ellis went to the gallows for shooting dead her former lover outside a pub in Hampstead. In many countries this would have been treated as a *crime passionnel* with a much less severe sentence.

My mother returned looking very sad and she told us how gloomy the atmosphere had been. They had performed in the chapel and the prisoners were not allowed to clap so all they could do was hold their hands together as a sign of appreciation. One of them afterwards told her how much pleasure they had brought to this terrible place. It touched her greatly, for although she was a firm believer in the old biblical eye-for-an-eye, like so many others at that time, she had been deeply moved by Ruth Ellis's plight.

Golders Hill Park with its menagerie of small animals and the adjoining Hampstead Heath were very much a part of my childhood. Visiting the wallabies and deer, cooing over the rabbits and feeding the ducks, these are memories I still hold fondly in my mind. The heath was the site of the famous bank holiday funfair – a long-standing, thrice-yearly entertainment which, in those days, occupied not only the extensive site running from opposite Whitestone Pond towards the Spaniards Inn but extended right down the hill in the direction of South Hill ponds. The swings and carousels, the dodgem cars and the ghost train together with throwing rings, trying to hook the floating 'ducks' and eating toffee apples and candy floss, are what made the fair so exciting. It was as though the 1920s were very much still alive on Hampstead Heath in the early 1950s; nothing had changed. People travelled miles to visit the famous Hampstead Heath funfair. We were lucky, living down the road at Golders Green, to have it on our doorstep.

To me, as a child, Golders Green seemed a well-ordered place where the local shops kept strict hours of opening and closed at lunchtime every Thursday for 'early closing'. Sunday shopping simply did not exist. There was Quibbels the chemist, Salmons the grocers and a hardware shop, the United Dairy and W.H. Smith – the only one of these still left seventy years on. W.H. Smith had at that time a distinctive style of interior decor with oak panelling and false crested opaque glass windows inside, leading in from an open-fronted area off the street where they sold the newspapers and magazines. Outside the adjoining bank stood Fred the paper seller with his three evening titles under his arm and his crutch by his side, one of the many old wounded soldiers from the First World War who were still much in evidence. '*Star*, *News* and *Standard*,' he would call out. On the corner of Hodford Road and Golders Green Road was where the nice lady with the flowers had her pitch.

As I started growing up, I was aware as a matter of course of being surrounded by the heavy guttural sounds of continental accents and foreign languages. Golders Green was a melting pot. Until the early part of the twentieth century, it had just been a country crossroads on the way between Hampstead and Hendon. Constable painted on many occasions the view from Hampstead across a sylvan valley to the distant spire on Harrow on the Hill. It is hard to imagine that this same setting is modern-day Golders Green and Hendon. Golders Green's turning point came in 1907 with the arrival of the Tube, the first railway to breach the Northern Heights, the high ridge surrounding north and north-west London. The Tube went underground, emerging from its tunnel just south of Golders Green Station. It brought prosperity to the area, which very quickly developed into a tree-lined modern suburb. Early on, it attracted the more affluent Jewish immigrant families who had started off in Whitechapel and the East End and were now looking to better themselves. Then in the 1930s came the refugees from Germany and Eastern Europe fleeing from the ravages of Nazi Germany. Everyone seemed to get on well together — you knew your neighbours and not just the ones next door. It was quite common to be sent round to ask to borrow a cup of sugar or some milk.

Growing up in the late forties and fifties was to experience the last vestiges of Edwardian living mingled with a dash of life from the inter-war years, the twenties and thirties. Although the way of life had become very different following the Second World War, some old habits clung on. In a fairly affluent area like Golders Green, some families still employed live-in maids as well as daytime help and the ladies of the household still organised afternoon tea, which was taken at home with their friends. A lamplighter appeared in our street morning and evening to extinguish and rekindle the gas streetlamps. Coal arrived in sacks on the back of a horse-drawn cart and the milkman from United Dairies came in a horse-drawn dray. The knife grinder and the French onion seller called at the door and the rag-and-bone man still yelled out his trade call as he trotted down the streets in his horse and cart.

There were very few places to eat in Golders Green and virtually none of these was licensed to sell alcohol. This was due, it was said, to the church commissioners owning the freehold of much of the land. The nearest public houses were by Hampstead Heath or towards Hendon. Supermarkets hadn't yet arrived and everything bought in a shop was handed over from behind the counter. Biscuits were weighed out from big tins, butter cut from large chunks and patted down to the requisite size and at Christmas the butcher's was festooned with what seemed like a fantastic array of turkeys and game birds hung both outside and within in great rows. Health and safety were not apparently of much concern then. Above all, there was rationing, sometimes more severe than it had ever been during the war and lasting right up past the coronation until 1954. Liberation from rationing when it finally came led to an orgy of sweet buying and over-indulgence such that the dentists of north-west London must have rubbed their hands in glee!

Opposite Rodborough Road, where we lived, on Finchley Road, was the Ionic, a little architectural gem and one of the earliest examples of a purpose-built cinema, dating from 1912. John Betjeman waxed lyrical about it but property developers were allowed to destroy it in the seventies and turn it into a supermarket. Fortunately that was not to be the fate of the Golders Green Hippodrome, although several attempts were made to close it. I remember collecting signatures as a child as part of a campaign to save it. It is still standing even though it sadly has not been used for live performances since 1968 when it was taken over by the BBC and used as a recording studio.

The Hippodrome was an imposing cream-coloured building right by the Underground station. It opened in 1913 providing the local, fast-growing population with entertainment and variety. In the days before television, and with a visit 'up to town' to see a show being something of a luxury, the local theatre thrived with a year-round programme of touring shows, pre- and post-London runs, musicals, opera and ballet and of course the annual pantomime.

My earliest memories of going to the Hippodrome are of pantomime. Max Wall, Jimmy Edwards and Max Miller were some of the pantomime stars I can remember and it was almost obligatory to go onstage with lots of other children at some special moment during the performance. In fact, all the big stars used to play panto at Golders Green and I must have seen many of them. When I was just a little older, my maternal grandmother started to take me on Saturday afternoons to the matinees. It cost two and sixpence (twelve pence) to sit in the gods on a wooden bench, with a reduced price for children. She loved musicals and operetta and she took me to see very many different productions.

The near-annual visit by the D'Oyly Carte Opera Company introduced me to the world of Gilbert and Sullivan. Later, as I grew older, I was drawn to plays. It was then the custom for very many London-bound productions to include Golders Green as their last stop before a West End opening, in the days before previews were introduced. Likewise, many successful West End shows would begin their post-London tours at the Hippodrome.

It is hard to imagine what infinite variety and choice was available week by week, year in, year out, and I took full advantage of all that was on offer. Sybil Thorndike and Athene Seyler in *Arsenic and Old Lace*; Anna Neagle endlessly touring in thrillers; Topol in *Fiddler on the Roof*; Sheila Hancock in *Rattle of a Simple Man* and *The Anniversary*; Marlene Dietrich; Fonteyn dancing with Nureyev; Vanessa Redgrave in *The Prime of Miss Jean Brodie*. These are just a few reminiscences of an amazing almanac of productions and stars. In those days, the West End boasted a roster of 'names' which added greatly to the commercial value of a production when they were posted 'above the canopy'. As a London suburb, Golders Green was an easy place to get to and, with two thousand seats, a successful week at the Hippodrome could gross a large amount of money.

And so I became hooked, even though I did not quite know it. I loved the theatre, though I never thought of it as a potential career. Nobody from a middle-class family living in Golders Green could aspire to anything beyond a 'proper job' in one of the professions. Music and theatre were all very well but were quite definitely pastimes and certainly not a source of employment. Even though there was a strong musical thread running through my mother's family and a distinguished actor on my father's side, such things were beyond our world ...

The 1950s were a period of great change. The austere start to the decade gave way to a more affluent era encompassed famously in Prime Minister Harold Macmillan's phrase 'You've never had it so good.' The Festival of Britain at the start of the decade was the must-see event of 1951. To a grey London still full of bombed-out building sites, it brought colour and excitement in a way that the Millennium Dome never did. My memories are hazy but I can still see the Skylon and the Battersea Fun Fair, where I was too young to ride on the Big Dipper, although my elder brother did. I also remember going to the festival cinema which was showing a special presentation of 3D films. The Royal Festival Hall clearly did not register with me at the time.

After kindergarten, I was sent to the local primary school, Wessex Gardens, which I joined at the time of the coronation. For a whole year, the country went coronation mad. Everything was leading towards the great day, 2 June 1953. We learnt about every move of the ceremony, the duties of each of the great officers of state, the symbolism and majesty of the coronation service. At school, we were each given a coronation mug and a spoon. I now realise that it was easy for the country to organise everything so well. The late king, George VI, the queen's father, had had his coronation in 1937, only sixteen years previously, so virtually all the participants were still around for this next one. His father, George V, had been crowned in 1912 and his father, Edward VII, in 1902, so there were quite a lot of people who had been involved in three previous coronations over the preceding fifty years. Our present queen has reigned for nearly seventy years, so there is probably hardly anybody left with any direct knowledge of the coronation ritual.

When the day itself arrived, as we did not have a television at home, like so many others, we were invited to see the great event with friends who lived nearby. So I went with my parents to the Ockrents. I had been to kindergarten with Michael, their son, who incidentally went on to a distinguished career as director of *Me and My Girl* and *Crazy for You.* Sadly, he died aged only fifty-three from cancer. The coronation transmission, which started early and included carriage processions before and after the actual ceremony and much else besides, was scheduled to last for much of the day. At one point during the most sacred part of the ceremony, the camera panned discreetly to the top of the canopy under which the monarch was being anointed with sacred oil. The screen was thus filled with a view of a piece of decorated cloth. Michael and I asked why the ceremony had stopped and his father, a Jewish research chemist from Glasgow, told us in his broad Scottish accent, 'They're putting oil on the queen's titties,' which sent two seven-year-olds howling with delight whilst his wife remonstrated with him over his choice of language.

It was inevitable that we would eventually have a television of our own at home but my parents resisted for another two years. Meanwhile, radio was a hugely important part of our lives. *Children's Hour* occupied the five o'clock spot on the BBC Home Service, as it was then called. What was so magical about radio was that it stimulated the imagination of the young listeners. I still have those mental pictures of the characters in *Toytown* and *Jennings at School*.

Once, when I was listening with my brother, the programme was interrupted by the grave voice of an announcer with the news that Winston Churchill had resigned as prime minister. We called my mother and she recalled with tears in her eyes his great wartime service.

When my father did eventually purchase a television it was for rather self-indulgent reasons. We had been at a friend's house and had watched the first part of a new mystery drama series. He wanted to see the next episode and so splashed out over fifty pounds on a modest black-and-white set — it had to be black and white as colour was not then an option. He was determined that we would not be totally corrupted by television and so he did not take up the option to have a special aerial fitted which would have allowed us to receive the new independent television channel which had only just begun transmissions; we were a strictly BBC household.

At first, there was a complete shutdown after the children's television finished at six o'clock. Then came a breakthrough with *Tonight* introduced by Cliff Michelmore, which closed the gap with its weekday magazine style programme. The programme included the nightly calypso sung by Cy Grant and encompassed as much of the current news stories as could be fitted in. 'The Budget will soon be arriving, I hope I've a chance of surviving,' was one particular line I still recall, along with, 'Mr Macmillan said today that the Tory Party is here to stay,' and the inevitable final stanza, 'We bring you the news you ought to know in *Tonight*'s topical calypso.'

In 1955, we embarked *en famille* on a 'continental motoring holiday'. My dad had mapped out an incredible three-week trip across France, Belgium, Holland, Luxembourg, Germany, Austria, Switzerland and Italy. Just ten years after the war, at a time when few people went abroad, it was a bold step. We saw what to us at the time were incredible sights from Lake Garda in Italy to the Brenner Pass and the Grossglockner in Austria.

When we reached Bavaria, Dad saw on the map that we were not far from Berchtesgaden, Hitler's Eagle's Nest. He was quite unaware until we got there that it had been blown up and destroyed by the Americans at the end of the war. Disappointed at not being able to see this, he stopped at a nearby roadside restaurant, which was quite basic but full of seemingly hospitable and welcoming Germans. There were not many tourists around so I suppose we stood out as we huddled around our table. A man came over with very thick glasses; it was clear that he had been injured at some stage, almost certainly as a result of the war.

'You are English,' he said in a heavily guttural voice. 'Where are you from?'

'From London,' we replied.

He beamed. 'I have been in London,' he said. 'I bombed Pich-a-dilly.'

There was a stunned silence; the mood changed immediately. 'Eat up quickly,' ordered my dad. As we hurriedly departed, I heard my father muttering profanities under his breath.

At eleven, having passed the Eleven Plus, I gained a place at University College Junior School in Hampstead where my brother was already enrolled in the senior school and the headmaster had only recently committed suicide. I hated it, I knew nobody there and did not make friends easily. I wanted desperately to leave. With a lot of encouragement, I stayed the course, eventually settling down to the new routine.

At thirteen, I moved to the senior school. I got through my five O Levels, which were all that was needed in those days for entry to one of the professions. I did two further terms before being whisked away by my dad three days before my sixteenth birthday. The day I left, I returned in the evening to hear a performance by the school's Choral Society of Handel's *Messiah*. I had never heard it complete before. I did not realise then that it would become an important part of my future life.

CHAPTER THREE

'AN ARTICLED CLERK
I SOON BECAME'

The reason for leaving school a few days before my sixteenth birthday in April 1962 was simple: I was going to be articled. My dad had always expected that one of his sons would follow him into accountancy. My older brother showed no interest at all in the prospect, instead choosing medical school — with which of course no one could argue. And so the spotlight fell on me. I was simply pushed into it, but in the nicest possible way. Accountancy was considered a pukka profession; my dad had his own firm and so it was natural that I would want to follow on. I signed my articles, was offered four pounds a week and began work.

I had, at the same time as working in the office, to take a correspondence course. There was a set procedure and I had to submit work on a weekly basis. Young and undisciplined, I started badly and got steadily further and further behind. After eight months, I was six months behind with the correspondence course and even my father had to admit that it did not seem I was cut out for accountancy. After less than a year, he released me from my articles. It was a day of great sadness for him and my mother but for me, although I dared not show it, a moment of freedom and liberty.

My parents were in despair. One day, when my brother, Nicholas, brought a fellow student from Guys' Hospital round for dinner, my mother told him how proud they were of Nick. As I left the room, she pointed after me, saying, 'But as for him, we really don't know what to do.'

I didn't much know myself what I wanted to do. I knew that I did not want to do accountancy, that much was sure, but, at the same time, I was under a lot of pressure to get a 'proper' job. Even though my uncle's brother was an actor of some repute, the performing arts were not looked upon as real work. You had to have a qualification to rely on so that you could be guaranteed a living for the rest of your life. The vagabond life of a thespian, or indeed anything associated with the performing arts, did not fit this requirement, but conformity did not appeal to me in the least. I think I knew what I wanted – not so much as being able to define it but in much broader terms. I wanted to be free, to be my own master, to do something I really enjoyed. I was aware even then of the multitudes of people who only seemed to work in order to have time when not working to do the things they most enjoyed. I wanted to turn this on its head, to enjoy the time I was working and to hell with time off.

Rather at a loose end now I had been released from accountancy, I found myself spending a lot of time reading at the local library. They had available a copy of *The Stage* each week and the monthly *Opera* magazine. I also managed to get to the West End to see theatre a great deal and to the opera as well, at Covent Garden and Sadler's Wells, where the company was still based in its pre-English National Opera days. I saw almost anything I could, including a tribute concert to Benjamin Britten on his fiftieth birthday at the Royal Festival Hall on 22 November 1963. A special concert performance of Gloriana was being presented and Britten himself was in the royal box. Great applause greeted his arrival at the start and the audience settled down to listen to the performance. Peter Pears as Essex and Sylvia Fisher as Queen Elizabeth and a wonderful cast of British singers sang in what I believe was the first performance since the original run at Covent Garden in coronation year, ten years previously.

Unbeknownst to the hushed audience listening to the tale of the Virgin Queen, several thousand miles away, in Dallas, a tragedy was unfolding. On the Underground on the way home I was surprised to see so many people reading that morning's papers. Then I realised that they were all early editions of the following day's papers, something I had never seen before. The headlines all bore similar copy – President John F. Kennedy had been shot at Dallas.

When I got home, my dad told me that Kennedy had died. It is hard to describe the impact of this tragedy. Kennedy was a young, brash, charming politician who had not only got America through the Cuban Missile Crisis a year earlier, when it really felt as if we could be on the brink of a third world war, but also brought a sense of youth to an otherwise grey world of old men. So his death really resonated through the generations in a way that might have seemed impossible if the victim had been somebody rather older.

Several months after I had thrown in the towel with my articles, I started a new job. Finding one had been a problem. I still had no real idea what I wanted to do – like many seventeen-year-olds I suppose – so my father had spoken to his friend and client Tommy Cummins, head of Pathé Newsreel. Could he find me a job? He probably created the one he offered me, which was rather more than I deserved.

I was to work as a general assistant at eight pounds per week and would be based at their offices in Wardour Street, centre of the film world. At the time, newsreels were still one of the main providers of news, but only just. Pathé, with two editions each week, was in the forefront of this declining industry which would soon be killed off forever by advances in television news reporting.

I joined just a few days after President Kennedy's assassination, which kept the news team busier than ever with the need to constantly update each edition to reflect the unfolding drama: the assassination itself, the arrest of Lee Harvey Oswald, the funeral of the president and Oswald's murder by Jack Ruby. The in-house commentator (and another client of my father's) was Bob Danvers Walker – the 'voice' of Pathé, the same voice that had provided such a distinctive touch to Pathé's wartime output when he demonstrated that even at the darkest moments, he could provide uplifting optimism with his presentation. John Stagg, the scriptwriter, had also been part of the wartime team. So there was still an extraordinary link with the great days of Pathé as one of the principal morale boosters of wartime Britain.

I also sat alongside a news editor whom I simply knew as John. It was only many years later, when I read his fulsome obituary in *The Times*, that I finally realised with whom I had been working. He was the great cameraman John Turner, who filmed throughout the war, including the explosion and sinking of HMS *Barham* in 1941, though the footage was supressed by the government until the war was over. Turner also covered the Japanese surrender in Singapore and was the only newsreel cameraman in India at the time of Gandhi's assassination and covered the funeral.

My job was to scan all the papers each morning looking for potential stories for Pathé to cover. I also had to frequently check the teleprinter, which clacked away almost ceaselessly with its stories from around the world, just in case there was anything relevant. Monday I found was my most enjoyable day as I could read all the Sunday papers and tabloids, as well as broadsheets. I did sometimes find something to propose but it was never taken up.

Occasionally, I would find myself out on an assignment, assisting one of the cameramen. When veteran Labour politician Herbert Morrison opened the Strand underpass I was there holding a light and I once found myself in a similar position outside Downing Street when German Chancellor Ludwig Erhard was making an official visit. That was the ultimate excitement, otherwise the stories were much more routine. Two eighty-something-year-old ladies in Hemel Hempstead who had been thrown out of their house and whom we filmed in hospital; a visit to the Tower of London for some long-forgotten filler piece; a look, for whatever reason no longer remembered, at the Shell Building on the South Bank. Even I could tell that newsreels had had their day and there was clearly not much future in all this. Moreover, I was bored; there was no stimulus, no encouragement and everyone involved seemed to recognise just as I did that the end for newsreels would not be long in coming. So, much to my parents' distress, I handed in my notice and embarked on a period of unemployment.

A couple of years before I joined Pathé, my father had formed the Mozart Lovers' Opera Society in order to stage a concert performance of *Cosi Fan Tutte* at the Rudolph Steiner Hall near Baker Street. It was not very clear why he wanted to do this other than that he loved Mozart. The evening raised money for Imperial Cancer Research. The following year, he became more ambitious and wanted to stage Mozart's *Il Seraglio*, which, at the time, was not very frequently performed. Somebody suggested he book St Pancras Town Hall on Euston Road opposite King's Cross and St Pancras stations. It had established itself as something of an operatic venue with the founding in the 1950s of the St Pancras Festival. This was an extraordinary initiative by an inner-London borough and shows the breadth of what could be achieved at that time by a local authority. Here they were sponsoring unknown operas and creating work for artists and musicians. Joan Sutherland sang Handel's *Alcina* at St Pancras Town Hall before achieving enormous success a couple of years later in 1959 in Donizetti's opera *Lucia di Lammermoor* at the Royal Opera House.

My dad's initial enquiry led to him being put in contact with Leonard Marcus, the deputy borough librarian and a largely unsung hero behind the pioneering work being undertaken at the festival during the 1950s and 60s. Leonard Marcus encouraged him to move forward with the project and gave him the free use of the hall. He also introduced him to a director, Rowland Holt Wilson, who had experience of putting together productions for the hall. Which was just as well, as my father knew absolutely nothing about this and needed guidance throughout. It was all done on a shoestring – ah, I hear some of you saying, so nothing changes. There were to be two performances with an amateur orchestra and chorus but professional soloists. My father had taken it into his head that he could play the speaking role of the Pasha Selim. He might have looked the part but he certainly had no stage experience and he would have been a disaster. Fortunately, the conductor, Fred Marshall, had worked for many years at the Old Vic and had numerous actors amongst his drinking companions. One of these, David Dodimead, was luckily 'resting' at the time and was to prove an excellent choice for the part.

Rowland had the idea to close the opera by sending the two happy pairs of lovers back home from Turkey via balloon, so the final tableau would be of them as they floated upwards in the basket as the curtain closed. But where to find a suitable balloon basket? Then he remembered that recently two intrepid British explorers had made the first balloon flight across Africa – Anthony Smith and Douglas Botting. Rowland was able to track Anthony Smith to his house in Primrose Hill. So one morning, by appointment, we went to an address in Elsworthy Terrace where we met not only Anthony Smith but Douglas Botting as well. They were extremely kind and were intrigued by the idea of using the balloon basket on stage. So not only was our balloon basket secured with the minimum of effort, it was also an enormous pleasure to shake the hands of two really pioneering explorers.

The performances sold moderately, despite my best efforts to market tickets amongst my parents' group of opera-loving friends. This time, there was no surplus to pay over to charity. Indeed, there was a substantial loss which my father had to pay out of his own pocket and my mother saw to it that he put an end to his ambitions to stage anything else. But I had loved the whole experience. My parents loved music, but as a hobby. This had allowed me to rub shoulders with performers and others involved in the music business — people whose lives and work were removed from our middle-class life in Golders Green. Now I was hooked and I knew it.

As I was quite good with my hands and had always liked woodwork, I had enjoyed helping to make the scenery for the production. Subsequently, when somebody asked whether I would be willing to help with making props for an opera at the St Pancras Festival, I was only too happy to agree. Gradually I got to know some of the people involved in the fringe opera groups around London and this led to my being asked to make the scenery for the Hintlesham Festival.

Hintlesham, in Suffolk, is set amongst some of the loveliest countryside in East Anglia. Hintlesham Hall on the edge of the village was then the home of an eccentric gentleman called Tony Stokes. He had been persuaded to start a festival there in the early 1950s as a diversion for him following a well-publicised divorce case. It was rumoured that he had paraded naked on his estate pulling a caravan and that any of his tenants who came and jeered at him had their rents reduced. I never discovered whether this was actually true but it certainly could have been.

The opera productions took place on a wooden stage set behind the large rectangular garden pond. This was drained each year and provided a perfect pit for the orchestra. Except that one year he delighted in turning on the fountains whilst the orchestra was in situ, which led, not surprisingly, to a walkout by the musicians. His eccentricities were widely known.

I found myself living in an idyllic setting in the house with peacocks roaming the gardens for three weeks while making the sets for *The Marriage of Figaro*. Tony Stokes treated me as one of the family. 'Do you share my liking for crab?' he might say and I would nod wisely as if I had always indulged in what were for me quite exotic tastes. I was blissfully happy; I was finally doing something I really enjoyed.

The festival was due to open on the Saturday. On the Friday, I caught a toad in the garden and put it in a jar. I'd had an idea and I just wondered if I dared try it out. Tony Stokes always expressed great admiration for Glyndebourne and the Christie family. He fancied himself as running something almost as important at Hintlesham. Each year, he invited George Christie to attend but, as far as I know, he never did. With my toad, I thought I might bridge the gap between Glyndebourne and Hintlesham.

I carefully added grass to the jar in which the toad was held and I drilled holes in the lid to provide air. Then I prepared a label which bore the legend 'Live Japanese Grass Frog — Groves of Marchmont Street, London WC'. I packed the jar into a cardboard box and sealed it carefully with tape. When I was certain that Tony Stokes was in his study at the hall, I nipped down to the telephone box in the village. I rang the number, making sure to press button A in advance of his answering the call (this was the old-style type of box long since phased out) so that when he answered he would not hear the coins fall.

'Hello?' he said in the clipped manner so instantly recognisable.

'Telegram for Mr A. Stokes,' I said, trying to put on a Suffolk accent that must have sounded suspicious.

'That's me,' he said. 'Can you read it to me?'

'Yes, sir,' I replied. 'It's dated today at 12.22pm and has been sent via Lewes. Message reads: "Unable to accept your kind invitation to festival opening STOP am sending small gift of appreciation to fellow gourmet on 3.45 to Ipswich STOP good luck with festival STOP George.'"

'That's George Christie from Glyndebourne, you know,' he said rather excitedly.

'That's as well may be but we'll send you down a copy later,' I said and hung up.

Some kind person gave me a lift to Ipswich and the man in the parcels office agreed, with a certain amount of financial persuasion, to mark the box down as having arrived on the 3.45pm train from London. Later that day, Tony Stokes sent somebody down to the station to collect the parcel.

The next day, the official opening took place with the Lord Lieutenant as guest of honour. Tony Stokes made a speech and, towards the end, he held up the jar containing the toad. 'My good friend George Christie from Glyndebourne cannot be here today but he has sent me this special gift.' Everyone nodded approvingly. Afterwards, the Lord Lieutenant was overheard to remark, 'Jolly nice of old George to send that. They're very rare, you know.'

At the first performance of *The Marriage of Figaro*, Tony Stokes spent much of the interval with an old-fashioned fly spray, squirting quantities of fly killer along the front rows of the audience. My dad, who had come with my mum to see the performance, introduced me to Anthony Asquith the film director and son of the First World War prime minister who was also in the audience and whom my dad knew through his work for the ACTT, the film technicians union. It transpired that he lived nearby and was well acquainted with Tony Stokes's entertaining if idiosyncratic foibles.

During my father's production of *Il Seraglio* in St Pancras, I had become friendly with the director and the conductor. Sometime later, after I had started working for Victor Hochhauser, we decided to form a company together to stage operas at the St Pancras Festival and anywhere else that would take us. Rowland Holt Wilson had worked at Glyndebourne and had also directed a number of opera productions at St Pancras and elsewhere. His family came from Suffolk and he had useful contacts with both Hintlesham and the newly restored Theatre Royal at Bury St Edmunds. Fred Marshall, the conductor, was working on a new realisation of Monteverdi's *Return of Ulysses*, then virtually unknown. With a grant from St Pancras Metropolitan Council, we were able to mount *Ulysses* at the festival in 1964 and it was very well received. One of the small tenor roles was sung by a young graduate, Roger Norrington. Now Sir Roger, a revered conductor, he was then just at the start of his career and was singing rather more than conducting. Creating a new company was an exciting prospect and I relished the opportunity to be in on the ground floor, right at the start. I was a quick learner and enjoyed the camaraderie that is so much a part of backstage life. To this day I cannot enter a hall or theatre without feeling my pulse quickening and a growing sense of excitement and anticipation.

Mr Hochhauser had given me time off to deal with the production. Now, a few months later, I had left his employ and was back running the company, albeit with no salary. We had been emboldened by our success with *Ulysses* and so we decided on staging three one-act operas by Hans Werner Henze the following year. I am not quite sure why we happened upon this trio of very contemporary works. I think the conductor and the director thought they would be challenging, interesting for the critics and that they would put us on the map. I realised quite early on how wrong they were but I lacked the gravitas to challenge my two vastly more experienced colleagues. I did, however, get to meet Henze in Rome when we were preparing for the production.

One of these pieces called for a dwarf and so we set about finding one. We were eventually recommended to hear someone who was then appearing in *Snow White on Ice* at Wembley. He came to audition and sang 'This Is My Beloved' from *Kismet* in falsetto. The shock of hearing him sing with his head voice caused me to have to leave the room; it was very unexpected. I quickly recovered my equilibrium and it was a very useful lesson in how to be prepared for any situation during auditions. We cast him and he did very well, except that at the second and last performance something occurred in the very narrow wing space at St Pancras Town Hall. Vince, a tall Irish stagehand, suddenly felt a hand reach up from below and, looking down, he saw our dwarf with a big grin on his face. It was just as well it was the final performance.

The St Pancras Festival organisers decided that after two years it was time to give somebody else a chance. Either that, or they had found the Henze works to be as boring and pretentious as I had. So, for the following year, we had no new production to look forward to. Then, out of the blue, came the offer to stage *Dido and Aeneas* at Hintlesham, where I had been so happy two years earlier. We even managed to engage the Northern Sinfonia to play for this, but putting on opera did not produce any money with which to run our new company.

Talking one day to a tenor friend, I had the idea of putting on a tour of Gilbert and Sullivan concerts, just four singers and a pianist. I mentioned this to Neil Duncan, the deputy director of the North East Arts Association, which was at the time the first and only such association in the country. I do not exactly remember how I had first met Neil but it turned out to be a fortuitous occasion which really set me on my way. Each year, the NEAA organised tours for its local amateur-run member societies. Generally these were located in small towns in Durham, Northumberland and North Yorkshire and each would put together an annual programme of events. Neil asked me to plan a 'package' which he could offer at the annual planning conference and that is how the Gilbert and Sullivan evening came about.

John Cameron, our country doctor in the Henze opera of that name, was associated with Gilbert and Sullivan, having sung several of the roles on Malcolm Sargent's EMI recording series. He also made regular appearances at Sargent's Gilbert and Sullivan prom night. He readily agreed to headline our tour and the NEAA came up with ten or so performances. I was able to extend the tour by adding dates at either end on the way up north and back south and soon had a tour of twenty or more dates. I then began to wonder why I was putting together the commercial arm of our company whilst still not being able to draw a salary. All the money to be made on the tour was already earmarked to pay off past debts incurred by the operas. Then it struck me — why not, I asked myself, set up on my own?

CHAPTER FOUR

GOING IT ALONE

O nce I had decided to start out on my own, I set about finding work. As I had discovered from the success of the tour for the North East Arts Association that there was a market for the Gilbert and Sullivan evenings, this seemed a good lead to pursue. The Theatre Royal at Bury St Edmunds invited me to present two performances there on 21 and 22 October 1966. This original Georgian theatre, first opened in 1819, had recently been brought back to life, having been used for many years as both a furniture store and brewery warehouse. It was rather like a miniature opera house with a horseshoe balcony with little boxes; in all, it seated not much over three hundred. The four soloists included a rather good young tenor, Philip Langridge, who appeared in dozens of my early concerts before moving on to a distinguished international singing career.

I arrived in the late morning and was having lunch near the theatre when I heard the terrible news on the radio of the Aberfan disaster – a school had been buried beneath a tip of colliery waste, which had collapsed. One hundred and sixteen children died and many adults too. There was talk as to whether we should cancel the performance but the theatre decided it should go ahead. A vicar said prayers before the start; it was a strange beginning.

I somehow managed to preserve the box office returns from those first two performances, which is strange because I have managed to retain very little paper ephemera from those early days. The returns show the cash takings and the number of seats sold at each price for every performance. The Friday evening sold 203 tickets and took £74 13s 6d (£74.67) and the Saturday performance 231 tickets and £112 9s 0d (£112.45). Somehow, I had managed to make a profit. The fact that these were the very first performances I had promoted in my own right and that the two performances had managed to cover costs and make a small profit was of great significance to me. If the takings had been smaller, leading to a loss, it might have depressed me at a very important juncture. That I had actually made money was a great spur. Being at a theatre, producing my own show was something very special and set me on the road I was to follow for decades to come. It really was the start of a great adventure. I felt confident at that point that I would have enough work for six months. After that — well, who could tell?

I started by working from my parents' home, where I was still living, but I really wanted an office in order to establish myself properly. Wandering down Oxford Street one day, I saw a 'For Rent' sign outside Dryden Chambers at 119 Oxford Street. I was in luck — the lettings manager told me he had one small room available at £150 a year. I took it. In all, I stayed there for five years, eventually taking over an adjoining room as well.

Dryden Chambers was a rabbit warren of small offices, which until the war had all been flats with apparently a rather dubious reputation. One day, shortly before I moved from Dryden Chambers to larger offices in Tottenham Court Road, I arrived to find a film crew in the courtyard and there in one corner was the unmistakable shape of Alfred Hitchcock. He was filming Frenzy and whenever it is rerun on the television I always try to watch the opening few minutes which features shots of Dryden Chambers. It is like revisiting an old friend.

The original office was tiny, no more than one hundred square feet, but it was mine and my ideas would, I hoped, be a little bigger than the office. I put together three or four concert programmes and wrote round to all the smaller halls and theatres listed in *The Stage Yearbook* for 1966. Besides the Gilbert and Sullivan evening, I added a Viennese evening with Marion Studholme, one of the leading sopranos from Sadler's Wells Opera, as it was still then known. Viennese operetta was still very popular at that time and the Viennese evening was a variation of a well-tried formula, mixing the operettas of Johann Strauss and Franz Lehar with the music of Mozart and Schubert.

To this, I added something I called 'Songs from the Shows'. This was a selection of popular songs from the great musicals. At the time, this meant the American musicals of the post-war era, especially Rodgers and Hammerstein together with then perennial favourites like Sigmund Romberg's *The Student Prince* and *The Desert Song*, the musicals of Ivor Novello and of course Noel Coward.

This was not long after Harold Wilson had appointed Jennie Lee to be the very first Minister for the Arts. Until her appointment, there had never been any such role in the government. She pushed the boundaries and gave the arts a higher profile. During her tenure, there was enormous encouragement for local authorities to take over defunct or failing commercial theatres and to build their own civic halls and theatres. This brought opportunities for the wider arts establishment and helped to create the mid-1960s thirst for the arts, which I benefited from by being on the ground at just the right time with my small-scale concerts. The timing here was everything — right idea at the right time. Ten years earlier, there was no such government encouragement; ten years later and public taste had moved on.

And so, the small-scale events that I had were, just as I had hoped, welcomed by these venues, helping them to fill their programmes. I had found my market. Within days of sending off the letters, I started to get bookings. Cheltenham Town Hall took the Gilbert and Sullivan programme for a date in early January 1967 and then Rotherham Civic Theatre booked the Viennese evening followed by a three-night engagement at the Theatre Royal, St Helens. Every week, new bookings came in. I realised that there was the prospect of having a proper business.

I dealt with everything myself, from booking the artists to sending out the programme copy, publicity information and photographs of the artists to the venues. I had put on my first two concerts at the Theatre Royal, Bury St Edmunds, on a risk basis to me in that I received a share of the box office rather than on a guarantee or fixed fee. So it was quite bold of me to have taken the risk but it had paid off. Subsequently, however, I went for straight fees or, occasionally, as some of the venues got larger, on a guarantee on account of a percentage. There are many ways to skin a cat and just as many when it comes to sharing out the box office receipts.

Incidentally, the name 'box office' derives from the practice within Elizabethan theatres of the audience paying for entry by placing coins in a clay box. These boxes from the different points of entry were then taken to a central point in the theatre and then deliberately shattered into pieces. All the coins were gathered and counted, and the cast and whoever else was involved were paid their percentage of the takings. Simple, really, and thus the origin of our modern box office.

The fees I charged for the complete package were between eighty-five and one hundred pounds. This gave me a profit of between fifteen and twenty pounds a performance and I felt rich beyond belief; I was earning money and doing something I absolutely enjoyed. I was my own boss with nobody to order me about and all this at the age of just twenty. My dad had given me fifty pounds and I arranged to borrow a similar sum from the bank. Somehow, I managed to balance the books even though I was sometimes overdrawn. It helped that my father used the same branch; it made them more tolerant towards me which was very useful.

The Viennese evening proved so popular that for a time I had to put together two groups of singers to cover all the dates. I was dashing all over the place with copies of the British Railways timetable books always about my person to make sure it was all ticking along. While Marion Studholme and the team were already engaged with performances in one part of the country, I formed a second group headed by Victoria Elliott to service the others. A real diva from Sadler's Wells Opera, she took command of the stage and marshalled the other two singers and the pianist with military precision. At the end of each performance when they were taking their final calls together, she had a wonderful knack of taking the two male soloists ostensibly by the hand but actually by the wrist. Then, standing centre stage, she would make as if to draw them both towards her in a line up while, with brute strength, actually pushing them back so that she stood out in front of them both. An old theatrical trick I suppose. The audience never noticed and the other singers took it all in good humour. I was learning so much and so quickly.

The Theatre Royal, St Helens, was a really interesting venue. Acquired by Pilkington Glass, one of the biggest employers in the area, it was funded and run by them for the benefit of the local community. I got to know the manager, James Lovelace, very well. An experienced operator who had been running theatres for many years, he had been brought in to run the

....

Theatre Royal with more or less a free hand. He loved my concerts, which could generally sustain a three-day run at the theatre – a bit of a luxury for me and the artists. Later on, he encouraged me to put together a recital series which he underwrote and I remember performances with Elizabeth Schwarzkopf and Victoria de los Angeles amongst others. This was symptomatic of the times – a burgeoning circuit of smaller theatres and halls which assembled interesting and broad-ranging programmes for local audiences. Many of these were 'civic' or 'municipal' venues run directly by the local authority. Those that survive are now very largely run indirectly by private companies and rely on a combination of tribute bands and alternative comedy performers. A far cry from those pioneering days of now more than fifty years ago.

Indeed, looking back, this really was a golden age. An awakening of civic pride, the idea that every municipality, however small, could and should provide entertainment as part of its civic duty. This was particularly important given the wholesale closure immediately prior to this time of theatres all over the country. In the mid-to-late 1950s, television had taken over and the effect on the regional theatres was profound. Some noble examples exist to this day but very many were demolished, converted to bingo halls or mothballed.

In the summer of 1967, I booked three Sunday evenings at the Palace Pier Theatre, Brighton. The deal was a split of box office receipts with the theatre and I also had to manage the press advertising, which had until then not normally been my responsibility. We started the series with the Gilbert and Sullivan evening, which made a profit of £150 pounds; I was beside myself with joy as this was a fortune. Also, I'd had the enormous pleasure of sitting in the box office during the Sunday afternoon helping to sell the tickets, my tickets.

Back then, a lot of the business was done on the day itself and when people asked for the prices I quickly learnt the trick of clearly articulating the top two prices and mumbling the lower two. It worked a treat; most people were too embarrassed to ask me to repeat the prices for a third time and therefore usually settled for the more expensive seats.

By now, I had amassed a regular group of artists that I used for the three shows I had begun with and was adding more shows as I grew in confidence and knowledge of what the audiences in these theatres around the country wanted. Because the level of work was increasing all the time, the artists all tried to keep themselves free for my dates. Of these, the one I booked the most was John Heddle Nash. I had first started working with him when John Cameron – who had headlined our original North East Arts Association tour – asked to be released from three concerts on the original 'Evening of Gilbert and Sullivan' tour and his agent had suggested Nash as a replacement. He had been a stalwart of the old Carl Rosa Opera Company and more recently a leading singer with Sadler's Wells Opera. He also bore a famous name; his father was Heddle Nash, one of the best-known English tenors of his generation. People were forever mixing John up with his father – 'He still looks so young' was a frequent comment. He bore it all like a martyr. Of course, he did not have to carry Heddle as part of his professional name, he could have been known simply as John Nash. Somehow, I think he rather liked the martyrdom.

He and I got on very well and I was soon able to offer him lots of work heading not only the Gilbert and Sullivan evenings but also the musicals evenings, 'Songs from the Shows'. John acted as a genial host and compere as well as leading the small group of singers – four in the Gilbert and Sullivan evenings and just three in 'Songs from the Shows'. In the late 1960s, he was probably doing close to one hundred performances a year for me all over the country. We went back to the north-east on several occasions, including one tour where we were able to base ourselves in Middlesbrough for several days and drive out each day to the appropriate venue. I happened to be staying in the room next to his and was surprised when I woke up during the night to hear his voice on the other side of the partition wall. I strained to hear what he was saying and then I caught it: 'Good evening ladies and gentlemen, and welcome to our evening of Gilbert and Sullivan ... ' Ever the perfectionist, he was running through his links for the show. I looked at my watch; it was 5.45am.

An occasion that I particularly recall from those early days was an opera night at the New Theatre, Cardiff. The wonderful tenor Alberto Remedios was free and suggested James Lockhart as the accompanist. Then came the real bonus, for when I met with Jimmy Lockhart he indicated that Margaret

Price, the great Welsh diva, might be available. I was thrilled and couldn't believe my luck – I had a fantastic line-up and the theatre was delighted. It was only later that I learnt that Jimmy and Margaret were having an affair and the chance of a night away in Cardiff was too good to miss.

It was about this time that the 'Furney' verse was born in the Gilbert and Sullivan evenings. As the tenor soloist was about to go on stage to sing 'Take a Pair of Sparkling Eyes' from *The Gondoliers*, one of the other singers said, 'Don't forget the Furney verse,' which meant nothing to him (or me) at the time. However, once he got to the second verse, it suddenly all became clear with the line, 'Furnish it upon the spot ... ' He got a fit of the giggles, which you might do too if you articulate it as he did, 'Furni-sh it upon the spot.'

One of these performances was scheduled for the James Finnegan Memorial Hall at Eston, just outside of Middlesbrough itself. John used to drive himself and I would take the other soloists and the accompanist in my car. On this occasion, John asked if he could follow me and we left the hotel at about five o'clock for the short hop to Eston. I could see John driving behind me round the ring road until just after one roundabout when I checked in the mirror and found he was no longer there. I hung back for a while but he did not reappear. The traffic was heavy and I assumed that he had got stuck behind a truck. We arrived at the hall, which was locked and, trying the door, we could hear the incessant ringing of a telephone.

Opposite was a pub that had just opened for the evening. We all had a drink and, after a little while, the two lady soloists went across to see if the hall was open as they needed to start preparing for the concert. One of them came running back, 'Ray, you must come quickly. John's wife was on the phone – John's had an accident.'

I rushed over to the hall and called her back straight away. 'John's in the General Hospital; he's all right and says he will be able to go on but can you go to collect him?' she said.

Somehow I found my way to the hospital and discovered John in the casualty department suffering cuts and bruises but otherwise quite cheery. On the way back to the hall, he told me that he had found himself, whilst following me, driving across the middle of a roundabout instead of round it. He had ended up in the flowerbeds and his car was a write-off.

We arrived in ample time for the concert but John insisted we start fifteen minutes late and that, of course, we make an announcement. So I found myself going on at the start to explain that John had been in an accident but, true professional that he was, he would go ahead with the show. This drew great applause and John hobbled on with a little more of a limp than I had been aware of when he left the hospital. He perched on a barstool on the stage instead of going off for the items when he was not singing and he had the audience in the palm of his hand. At the end of the performance, he got massive applause before the audience moved off towards the exits at the back of the hall. Then I noticed that there were two figures moving forward, against the flow. When they emerged at the front of the stage, I could see that they were policemen. John hobbled across from his stool towards them.

'Mr Heddle Nash,' one said, 'what a pleasure to meet you. I must caution you that anything you say may be taken down and used in evidence against you.' John was charged with dangerous driving and subsequently had to pay a heavy fine.

Within twelve months of starting out on my own, the number of concerts had multiplied to the point where I was arranging well over 120 concerts a year. Considering that, when I started, I had imagined there would be enough work for six months, I did not feel I was doing too badly. The concerts took me all over the country and I very soon got to know the journey times from London to Cornwall, from Hadrian's Wall to the south coast and from Norwich to west Wales. The map of the UK that I had hung on my office wall in Dryden Chambers was soon covered in dozens and dozens of coloured dots marking the towns and cities where we had performed. England, Scotland and Wales were all represented, though Ireland – both Northern and the Republic – remained virgin territory. I even managed a visit to the Orkneys and Shetland Islands with the Gilbert and Sullivan concert with an appropriately Scottish opera star, Ian Wallace, heading the singers. Ireland did follow eventually when I took the Johann Strauss Gala to the RDS Hall in Dublin. Then, when the National Concert Hall opened in the old university buildings, the floodgates opened and it became a regular port of call.

I continued to do everything myself, a veritable one-man band. At times it was very busy and led to one moment of deep embarrassment which still makes me shudder whenever I think of it. I had taken an engagement at the

Royal Theatre, Northampton. The booking was for a Viennese evening on the Monday night followed by a Gilbert and Sullivan evening on the Wednesday – or at least that is what I thought it was. We played the Monday; it went very well and nobody at the theatre said anything when I waved a cheery goodbye at the end and said, 'See you Wednesday!'

The next evening, just after seven o'clock, I had a telephone call at home from Mr W. Bland Wood, the general manager of the theatre. 'Where are your artists?' he asked rather pointedly. It seems we were expected to do two Viennese evenings, not just one. It was then too late to do anything about it and the audience had to depart without the soft refrain of 'Vienna, City of Dreams' ringing in their ears. I carefully checked the correspondence and it was never made clear that a second show was being considered. Anyway, the theatre was very nice about the whole thing and my red face the next day should have told them how deeply sorry I was. The Gilbert and Sullivan evening went very well but I do not think we ever got a repeat booking at the theatre.

I have never had anything like that happen again, though I did come close, once, a few years later, when the conductor Marcus Dods called me. He had noticed that he was listed in the South Bank diary to conduct the following month at the Queen Elizabeth Hall – I had forgotten to book him but fortunately he was free.

CHAPTER FIVE

OH, I DO LIKE TO BE BESIDE THE SEASIDE

It is hard to imagine when looking around some of the country's most deprived areas along the coast that these were once thriving, vibrant communities for whom the annual summer season was of vital importance. For almost three decades after the end of the war, the British summer season flourished but the arrival in the early 1970s of the affordable package holiday that whisked people off for seven days of guaranteed sunshine on the Costa Brava finally sounded the knell for the traditional summer season. Who would willingly go for two weeks to Blackpool where an old harridan of a landlady would shoo you out after breakfast, whatever the weather, and not let you back until it was time for 'high tea' when you could now fly off for seven days of Mediterranean sunshine?

Right through the fifties and sixties, the British seaside was a hugely important marketplace for summer shows and Sunday concerts. Blackpool would have ten or so major shows running right through the summer; Great Yarmouth was another major summer entertainment centre, as were Scarborough, Bournemouth, Brighton and so on, all around the coast. Eastbourne, whose new Congress Theatre opened in 1964, would host seasons of fifteen weeks. Indeed, it was Eastbourne that gave me a lucky break, moving me on a notch or two.

George Hill was the theatre's much-respected entertainments director and very influential amongst the municipal entertainment hierarchy. He first gave me a Sunday date in June 1967 for my Viennese evening, which was to prove a very positive imprimatur on my work, leading to bookings at many other coastal resorts and providing me with a lot of work throughout the summer and beyond. The phrase 'municipal entertainment' will not mean much nowadays but it is worth recalling that in the pre-Thatcher era nearly every local authority had its own entertainments officer and there was even for a time a flourishing monthly magazine called *Municipal Entertainment*. Many of the seaside venues were run by the local authority who had the responsibility of making sure that the town's entertainment venues were programmed to attract holidaymakers to the resort.

Most of these seaside resorts had changed little since their Victorian and Edwardian heydays. The piers, the amusement arcades, the candy floss and the fish and chips. Happy children with buckets and spades, mums and dads enjoying the beach and elderly grandpas with rolled-up trousers and braces and a knotted handkerchief for a sun hat. They enjoyed what sunny days there were, went to the amusement arcades when it rained and poured into the theatres for their evening entertainment.

The Stage, the industry's own newspaper, often used to feature advertisements from out-of-work performers seeking employment, largely in pantos or summer shows. They dressed these up with an introduction such as, 'Unexpectedly vacant between ... ' It was the raw, insecure side of the business which haunted everyone. And yet many an artist from that era was able to make a decent – if precarious – living moving between pantomime at Christmas and summer shows.

Blackpool really was the queen of resorts with some pleasant seafront hotels and acres of boarding houses in the mean streets running behind, all with reversible Vacancy / No Vacancy signs in the windows. The season could run from the late May bank holiday through to early autumn. On the other side of the country, on the North Sea coast, sat Scarborough, which fulfilled much the same function as Blackpool. Eastbourne on the south coast regarded itself as a cut above the rest and the Congress Theatre was a great addition to the town, enabling it to host touring productions of ballet, musicals and plays all year round. Bexhill, just along the coast, was known as 'God's waiting room', but Eastbourne with its elderly population was a close second. There was a genteel atmosphere, as though they were living several decades behind the rest of the country. Agatha Christie's Hercule Poirot would have felt quite at home here with the tea rooms and rather nice hotels stretched along the seafront made all the more pleasant without the commercialisation of nearby Brighton.

The Fol de Rols, which had originated out of the Pierrot shows popular at the turn of the twentieth century, was very popular in Eastbourne. It carried on the concert party tradition but with imaginative production. It was very much an ensemble company without big star names but it had built up a reputation and a following that was still very strong. The inevitable happened in 1968 and it was dislodged by *The Black and White Minstrel Show*, which had become all the rage on television. Quite how this contemporary adaptation of the old concert party routine of blacking up became so popular for a time is nowadays hard to imagine. The very thought of anyone putting on black face make-up, let alone an entire company doing so, now seems totally abhorrent. Yet they played to packed houses night after night. What was once quite normal, is now, thankfully, totally unacceptable.

I was walking to the station in Eastbourne on one of my frequent visits there when I came across a polished brass plate on an imposing villa. 'Dr John Bodkin Adams' was boldly engraved on it – a name which immediately conjured up a notorious case from the late 1950s when the doctor was put on trial at the Old Bailey for murder of one of his patients. It seems that the good doctor had received many bequests from amongst the hundreds of elderly lady patients who died, usually in a deep coma, not long after altering their wills. Seemingly against the odds, he was found not guilty. It subsequently emerged that he had friends in high places, extending right up to the Lord Chief Justice.

In Bournemouth, I was introduced to Max Bygraves, starring in his own summer show at the Winter Gardens. His supporting acts included a pair of pianists dressed as tailor's dummies and playing just as leadenly. 'What did you think of Rostal and Schaefer?' Max asked me. 'Absolutely wonderful,' I replied.

At Bridlington I saw the great Les Dawson. Now, he really could play the piano badly as part of his act but in his case it was intentional and he had a wonderful line in comedy. Bruce Forsyth, Jimmy Tarbuck, Val Doonican, et al. – I saw them all in my travels round the seaside towns for my Sunday concerts.

One of the most difficult places to get to was Llandudno. We used to drive almost everywhere and my car was always filled with the performers I was taking around the circuit. In those days, the M1 and the M6 had not yet been joined together and what is today a short section of motorway then involved a tortuous nearly two-hour drive on single carriageway roads, bridging the gap between the two motorways. At Llandudno, the Sunday concerts were run by and featured Robinson Cleaver, an organist and entrepreneur who also promoted the Monday to Saturday summer show. He always insisted on joining in somewhere during the programme, much to the annoyance of my regular artists who never knew when exactly he would decide to make his entrance.

I did once work with the really great organist Sandy Macpherson, whose wartime broadcasts had helped to keep the nation cheerful in dark times. He was quite old when I engaged him but absolutely full of life and even more so after a wee dram or two. He made his appearance onstage at the St George's Hall, Bradford, seated on the organ bench as it and the organ rose up through the stage floor on a lift. The cheering from the largely elderly audience was quite wonderful; he had them hooked before he had even played a note. From him and so many of that wonderful generation I learnt so much. They knew exactly how to work an audience for maximum effect. People like Sandy Macpherson were very kind to me, an unknown tyro still wet behind the ears but keen to learn. And I found I was a quick learner. I looked, listened and absorbed the knowledge and the lore associated with touring the British Isles.

Bournemouth was another wonderful seaside town, a cultured place with its own symphony orchestra and a range of venues. When I first started going there, it was presided over by Sam Bell, the likeable municipal entertainments director. He gave me a lot of work, rather like Eastbourne. My type of concerts seemed to suit his audiences and I was very happy when he kept adding dates. Later he was due to retire but, before he left, I noticed that forthcoming dates were not being confirmed beyond the 'pencilled' stage. So when I next saw him on a visit down there, I asked him about this.

'Oh,' he said, 'you'll want to put these through the new company I am forming with ... ' and he mentioned the names of a well-known booking agent and a prosperous local businessman, with both of whom he was clearly in financial cahoots. He expected me to take a fee and was creaming off a substantial margin between this and what he could charge the venue. As he controlled the diary and approved the contracts, he had a ready-made set up from the day he retired. There was not a lot I could do at the time although I subsequently managed to nudge everything back to normal by dealing directly with his successor.

I loved the seaside circuit — the wonderful sense of tradition, the satisfaction of arriving on a Sunday afternoon after a sometimes long drive across the country and returning the following day to London with the cheers of a (normally) full house ringing in my ears and hopefully a bit of a profit. Most of these venues had a resident stage manager, great characters, many of whom I got to know well over the years. They had experience and knowledge which they were happy to share. Badly paid and working long hours, they clearly loved their work. It is hard to explain how easily they could transform a grotty, cramped backstage area into a powerhouse for the evening's entertainment. How drab house curtains and drapes given suitable coloured lighting could quickly transform the stage into a magical focal point for an expectant audience. And at the end of the evening, they beamed with pleasure at seeing yet another satisfied audience show their appreciation as the performance came to an end.

At the height of the summer season, these venues came alive, becoming lively, crowded places of entertainment. There was an old-fashioned sense of simple pleasures enjoyed in the traditional, peculiarly British manner by generations of holidaymakers. For me, what could be more exciting than standing outside the theatre at Eastbourne at seven o'clock on a Sunday evening, watching lines of elderly patrons (or so they seemed to me at the time) arriving from all directions, some with walking sticks to help them along, all converging on the theatre for my concert? There was even a bonus when Ernest Fulcher, George Hill's deputy, added chairs to the side galleries to accommodate as many as possible of those who wanted to be there. Then I knew exactly why I loved this business; I positively tingled with excitement as the orchestra started the overture. We were under way.

I was now married with a lovely young daughter. Johanna, my wife, often used to accompany me to the series of Sunday concerts at the Pier

Theatre, Bournemouth. We would sometimes take little Emma, who was then two years old, with us, making a bed for her out of two chairs and some cot blankets in one of the dressing rooms. On the drive home she would settle down in the baby seat in the rear of the car. When she woke up, no matter where we were, we would say, 'Nearly home.' She got wise to this and soon learnt to reply, in a plaintive little voice, 'No nearly 'ome.'

Gradually, my work moved away from touring one-night concerts around the country to larger venues and the major London concert halls. So my journeys to the seaside grew less frequent and eventually slowed down altogether. By the time our second daughter, Louise, was born, in 1974, travelling around the country had more or less come to an end. Some years later, when I visited Bournemouth in the summer, I was shocked to find how much things had changed. 'The good old days' is a bit of a cliché but I really am glad I got in on the end of the seaside tradition before it changed so much. It was a real link back to a former golden age and it was a privilege to have touched that era, even at a distance.

CHAPTER SIX

LONDON CALLING

One of my leading soloists, Marion Studholme, introduced me to Donald Swann, the piano-playing half of Flanders and Swann who had had great success with their reviews *At the Drop of a Hat* and *At the Drop of Another Hat*, both in the West End and on Broadway. Described by one paper as 'the pixie-like prankster at the piano', Donald was an extraordinary character, a serious musician who was also a master of comic writing. His rather threadbare tenor accompanied Michael Flanders' deeper baritone in their huge range of comic material.

Donald had developed a programme of his own settings of various authors both old and contemporary, including some of J.R.R. Tolkien's works. He called the programme *Set by Swann*. Would I be interested, he asked, in booking dates for him? Besides Marion, there were two other soloists including her husband, Andrew Downie, and either Ian Wallace, the well-known Scottish operatic bass-baritone, or William Elvin, a young baritone whose name went remarkably well with the Tolkien material, some of which was written in Tolkien's made-up language of Elvish. I even got to meet the author himself at a launch party for Donald's songs organised by Tolkien's publishers, George Allen and Unwin.

I managed to put some dates together and then, with Donald's agreement, I decided to apply for a date at the newly opened Queen Elizabeth Hall on the South Bank. It was only because of Donald's reputation that I got allocated a date; they didn't know me from Adam and were initially very condescending. So, in September 1968, I presented my very first London concert, *Set by Swann*.

The hall was well filled and I comfortably covered the costs. I also liked the experience of promoting in London and vowed I would try to do more. Meanwhile, Donald was keen to take his show to America and so I wrote to various agents in New York and followed this up with a visit there, my first. I had an aunt who had lived there since the war and she was able to show me round. The sheer excitement and vitality captivated me; London seemed very tame by comparison.

Of the replies I received from the agents, the most promising was from Klaus Kolmar, then at the mighty William Morris Agency. He soon discovered that Donald Swann performing away from Michael Flanders was not an easy sell, but he managed to put together a tour of a dozen dates, mainly in universities but also including the newly opened National Arts Centre in Ottawa. The three performances there included one which they had sold on to the Kiwanis, a charitable organisation similar to the Rotarians. They were holding a convention in the city and this was their fun night out. Even before we started, Donald was startled by the raucous noises coming from the auditorium. 'You will bring down the curtain, won't you, if this continues during the show?' he said, quite seriously. I did not have the heart to remind him that he would be performing on an open thrust stage with no curtain.

In the event, his settings of Tolkien and Betjeman, Ronsard and Froissart seemed unexpectedly to please the audience and they ended up being quiet as mice during the performance and roared their approval at the finale. It was a good end to the tour that had started in Raleigh, North Carolina, in deep snow and uncertain travelling conditions. In fact, it almost did not start at all. When our plane from New York had landed at its previous stop, it was unclear whether it would be able to land at Raleigh, in which case it would have to overshoot and go on to the next stop a further hundred or so miles beyond. We decided to risk it and the plane was about to depart when Donald suddenly decided that he was going to get off. We all followed him looking rather embarrassed while the very good-natured pilot opened up the hold and himself searched for our luggage. We found a taxi at the airport willing to drive us the sixty or so miles to our destination and we got through only to find that the plane had indeed landed with no difficulty. The next town was Fargo, North Dakota, where the temperature was minus twenty and there was a railroad running across the main street, just as in all those old westerns. In all it was a short but effective lesson in overseas touring — fun when you are young.

Donald's rather wistful approach and sudden changes of temperament led us to call the show, behind his back, 'Upset by Swann' although it was not a fair comment at all. He was really charming; it is just that he had some strange programme ideas. I could not get too excited about his next project, *Evening in Crete*, with a Greek singer called Lily Malandraki, during which, I seemed to remember, he danced round the stage at one point à la Zorba the Greek. I knew I was onto a loser here when the theatre manager I was trying to interest in the show kept repeating, 'Lily Mala-who?' every time I mentioned her name. After that, I decided to concentrate solely on *Set by Swann*.

I had built my circuit of small-scale concerts into a thriving business with now as many as 175 dates a year. My work in London also started expanding but not without a struggle. The director of the South Bank was John Denison, a former horn player who had, prior to his arrival at the South Bank, been the music director at the Arts Council. His first wife (of four) was Anna Russell, the celebrated satirist of classical singing opera. John Denison, I later discovered, had been a military hero, landing on D-Day+1 and mentioned in dispatches. To me, however, he was a rather unbending and begrudging director who did not instinctively take kindly to a new kid on the block. Little by little, with perseverance and patience, I started to make inroads, much encouraged by Denison's deputy, George Mann, a kindly and paternalistic figure who was always keen to encourage new ideas. When John Denison retired, George Mann was promoted to director.

Promoting in London meant advertising in the national press. There was one advertising agency associated with the 'semi-display' advertising which most concert organisers used. Unlike full display ads, where the advertiser can arrange the layout at will and use different type styles and added illustrations, semi-display was a rigid, formulaic set-up. There were so many characters to a line and larger type could only be used for the title. Who could cope with this? Step forward Gosdens who specialised in exactly this type of advertising. Their Mr John Simpson was a past master at making best use of the limited space available, which had to be bought in those days by the column inch. Later I added my own logo, RG, and felt delighted to see this from time to time in the weekend press.

Gosden's suffered in the steep decline, over time, of the use of this sort of advertising and was taken over in circumstances that I cannot exactly remember by Simon Caradoc Evans, an endearing Welshman who gave the air of being largely a man of leisure. I got on well with him and liked him a lot. He invited my wife and me to see a performance of *Waters Round the Moon* starring Ingrid Bergman at the Haymarket Theatre. What's more, as he knew her well through a charitable foundation, he escorted us afterwards to her dressing room to have a drink with her. Images of *Casablanca*, *Anastasia* and *The Inn of the Sixth Happiness* flashed through my mind as we were introduced to her. An excellent play and a wonderful star.

This style of advertising had all but disappeared by the end of the 1980s. However, it was still going when I presented a Wagner Centenary Concert in 1983 at the Barbican with Alberto Remedios singing Walther's Prize Song, 'Rienzi's Prayer' and 'Winterstürme' from Die Walküre. The London Philharmonic Orchestra had suggested Karl-Anton Rickenbacher as conductor and he did a wonderful job. A little later I learnt that the LPO had proposed his name to Victor Hochhauser for one of his concerts for which they had been engaged. 'Karl-Anton Rickenbacker?' He said, 'The name is too long to fit onto one line in the ad; it will cost extra, we can't book him.'

The recent addition of the Queen Elizabeth Hall to the London scene came at just the right moment and enabled me to get a toehold into an otherwise almost impenetrable cartel. The Royal Festival Hall was rigidly programmed so that it was virtually impossible to be given a date there, especially as a new face on the scene, and the Royal Albert Hall was far too big for anything I might have to present. So the QEH with, at the time, eleven hundred seats, was ideal.

In the early days, I tended to present solo artists there. Ian Wallace gave his charming one-man show; I put on recitals with the English heldentenor, Alberto Remedios, and David Kossoff performed his very individual versions of Bible stories. However, I also wanted to try bigger events and in December 1971 I got my chance.

It was the one hundredth anniversary of Gilbert and Sullivan's very first collaboration, *Thespis*, a long-forgotten operetta for which nearly all the music has been lost. Only the lovely chorus, 'Climbing Over Rocky Mountains', which was reused by them in *The Pirates of Penzance* has survived alongside a single song. So I used the anniversary of the first staging of *Thespis* as the hook for a centenary concert, booked some of my regular artists, including Marion Studholme and John Heddle Nash, and was rewarded with a completely full house. I engaged Marcus Dods to conduct.

I had already worked with Marcus on some of the Viennese evenings in the larger venues. It was my good fortune that he was happy to do these early dates. He had enjoyed a very distinguished career as Muir Matheson's assistant on very many post-war film recordings. Matheson had been the doyen of conductors of film music, his name appearing on literally hundreds of films from the 1930s to the early 1960s. Marcus had been for a while musical director of the BBC Concert Orchestra and had worked extensively with Sadler's Wells Opera (later ENO). He was a brilliant musician and so easy to get along with. He was one of a number of people who really helped me to grow the business.

I even managed to get a good review in *The Times*, which for some reason had decided to cover the concert. As a result of this concert, the South Bank decided that I could be allocated the odd handful of dates each season at the QEH, starting the following September. Marcus and I discussed what we would do and planned a Viennese evening. I suggested we should fix our own orchestra rather than buy one in as we had done with the Gilbert and Sullivan centenary and so the London Concert Orchestra was born. I was now on my way to promoting regularly in London as well as all over the country.

Having started on my own in the swinging sixties, expanding the business in the soon-to-be very austere seventies was, with hindsight, something of a challenge. The post-war effect, so dominant a feature until quite recently, was finally vanquished. The economies in both West Germany and Japan were powering ahead, leaving us, so it seemed, far behind. Moreover, most of the remaining colonies and possessions forming the British Empire had at long last been given their freedom during the sixties. Rather more sadly, the last vestiges of the old coinage changed overnight in February 1971 with decimalisation. Gone forever was the tanner, the bob, the florin and the half-crown. The expression 'as bent as a nine-bob note' lost its resonance but adding up just pounds and pence was a lot easier than the hitherto three-column cash book of pounds, shillings and pence.

In 1973, the oil crisis following on the Yom Kippur War between Israel and the Arab coalition caused a massive hike in oil prices, cheap motoring vanished and oil-fired central heating became almost a luxury. Britain finally joined the European Community on 1 January 1973 and a subsequent referendum confirmed this. The following January, the Conservative government, led by Edward Heath, in an effort to break the power of the National Union of Mineworkers, introduced the three-day week, meaning electricity was only available to commercial users for three specific days each week.

By now I had a small number of employees, perhaps two or three. I never employed a large staff as I always found I could get by with a tight team. I had moved from Dryden Chambers in 1971 to larger premises in Tottenham Court Road opposite Maples, the very large furniture store, subsequently demolished and rebuilt as a much smaller store with several floors of offices above. We sat in a cold office for the other two days of the working week, when we had no power, with candles and torches. Places of entertainment were exempt so the show could go on but television ended abruptly each night at ten o'clock. Not surprisingly, the Heath government fell in February 1974 when Harold Wilson returned as prime minister in a minority Labour government. The decade continued with shaky national finances and periodic confrontations with the unions.

Throughout all of this really rather miserable period, I was building my business, promoting more in London and developing larger scale events alongside dealing with what would now be deemed as hyperinflation, with postal rates going up three times in a year, for example. Setting seat prices months ahead was quite a challenge, but I generally found that, despite the economic uncertainty, people still wanted to go out, to be entertained, to enjoy some escapism.

I was at long last getting odd dates at the Royal Festival Hall alongside the regular engagements I promoted at the Queen Elizabeth Hall. I was also finally in a position where I wanted to book dates at the Royal Albert Hall, though it was not, at first, easy to do so. Victor Hochhauser never liked the idea of anybody else putting on commercial concerts so he did his damnedest to block me whenever he could. He had considerable influence at the Royal Albert Hall in particular, which he used ferociously, doing his best to ensure that any dates I was offered were not prime days of the week. I had to accept that he would try to harm me. But here my predecessor at Victor Hochhauser's, Robert Patterson, was very kind and very helpful. He had become a really important promoter and booked the Albert Hall very regularly. So when he heard that I was having difficulty booking dates there because of 'outside influences', he used his not inconsiderable commercial clout to help me.

Unfortunately, Patterson's enormous success was to grind to a halt when he came a cropper with an Australian joint venture which went badly wrong. He had personally guaranteed the finances and he was eventually forced to sell his house to pay off the debts. He died aged only fifty-one and is now largely forgotten but I remember him with much affection as he went out of his way to help and encourage me. I even co-promoted with him just once, right at the end of his life. French flamenco guitarist Manitas de Plata was, in his heyday, a big star and Patterson had done lots of dates with him. We had one solitary date at the South Bank but it sold reasonably and we more than covered our costs. I rather wish I could have done more with Robert; he really was a major influence in the industry and very cordial and helpful to me.

It was around this time that I heard an intriguing story at the Royal Festival Hall. George Camp the backstage supervisor was, on first acquaintance, a rather gruff type who had clearly seen it all in his time. In fact, he turned out to be very helpful and kind to me once I got to know him. I was having a drink with him in the artists' bar at the hall when he told me about a visit he had had from the police. Actually it was officers from Special Branch and they were following up information about how the Soviet Union might have exfiltrated one of their agents. They asked George if he could provide them with a rigid harp case used by orchestras when touring overseas. Was it possible, they wondered, to substitute a person in place of the harp by providing a shelf to sit on within the case?

George obliged with a suitable case and they fiddled around for an hour or so with one junior officer having to assume the role of the spy and be packed up in the case. In the end they were satisfied that it could have been done and they were reasonably sure this was what had happened. George never discovered who they suspected but in those days there was seemingly no end of choice with 'reds under the beds' and other bizarre stories making regular appearances in the national newspapers.

The decade ended with the 1979 general election which brought Mrs Thatcher to Downing Street. One of the side-effects was the abolishment over time of almost all the old entertainments officers and directors' positions which were maintained by councils around the country. Venues were taken over by trusts, a few closed down or were converted to other uses and the pioneering spirit engendered by Jennie Lee in the sixties was swept aside. Overall I felt it was a great pity that the enthusiasm and financial support at local authority level was cast aside. The Arts Council continued to support major national and regional institutions but the involvement of the local authority in providing direct, local support was severely tested. The nurturing and progressive attitude which had enabled me to start up and expand in the sixties had evaporated.

CHAPTER SEVEN

RUSSIAN ROULETTE

Ever since I had left Victor Hochhauser and started up on my own, I'd had no dealings at all with Russian artists – indeed, I had had no real dealings with the Hochhausers either. However, after the success of the Gilbert and Sullivan centenary concert at the Queen Elizabeth Hall in December 1971, Victor Hochhauser got in touch to ask me if I could put together a similar programme for them at the Royal Albert Hall for one of their Sunday night concerts. I booked Ian Wallace, Marion Studholme and John Heddle Nash and a couple of other soloists but I made the mistake of asking if I could have proper billing alongside Hochhauser. Absolutely not, was the response – they had been promoting under their sole name for nearly thirty years! Although why that should have had such a bearing on my request I have no idea. So I had to be content with an acknowledgement on the title page of the programme.

On the night, as the artists were about to go onto the platform before a completely packed house, the tenor Edmund Bohan remarked to Victor Hochhauser: 'Look, it's a completely full house.' Never one to openly admit anything which might increase fees on another occasion, he instinctively answered with an enigmatic, 'It appears so.'

Around this time, the international community was becoming much more aware of the way the Soviets were treating their Jewish population, banning elements of Jewish culture and preventing many of those who wanted to from emigrating to Israel – these unsuccessful emigrants becoming known as 'refuseniks'. The protest at such treatment reached a certain crescendo with the case of Valery and Galina Panov, both leading dancers with the Kirov who were dismissed and later briefly jailed when they applied for exit visas to

Israel. They were also forbidden to take dance classes for two years, which, to active dancers, was virtually a form of torture. The wider plight of critics of the regime within the Soviet Union – including Aleksandr Solzhenitsyn, the great Russian novelist, and the nuclear physicist Andre Sakharov, a champion of human rights – was also very well reported in the international press. As a prominent member of the Jewish community, Victor Hochhauser was a clear target for criticism for continuing to deal with the Soviets and he was finding it difficult to continue working normally with the Russian companies with which he had long since had dealings.

Victor had booked the Georgian State Dance Company for a three-week season at the London Coliseum in the summer of 1973. Before it was publicly announced, I had a call from him, asking me to go and see him as he had something he wanted to ask me. Victor alluded to the problems they were encountering and then asked me whether I would manage the three-week Coliseum season and put it under the name of the small artists' management agency which I had at that time, called Tower Music. (The name, incidentally, was for no better reason than that I could see the top of the nearby Post Office Tower from the rear window at my office.) Victor said that it was better to use an impersonal name but I could not help feeling that he did not want me to do it under my own name as I might gain some outside benefit from this. So we agreed terms and, shortly afterwards, advertisements started to appear with the small acknowledgement, 'Season presented by Tower Music'. The Victor Hochhauser name was of course nowhere to be seen.

When the company arrived, we were all issued with backstage passes, the first time I had come across this now virtually essential procedure for venue security. The company rehearsed for a day and, when we all returned backstage after the lunch break, we found the stage crew laying large plywood sheets over the stage. It seemed that the Coliseum would not allow the Georgian men to throw their daggers into the stage, an impressive spectacle during a vigorous warrior dance.

Lillian Hochhauser had quite clearly not been consulted by her husband before he had agreed to the request to lay the plywood in order that this item in the programme could be performed as usual. 'Victor,' she said, 'why are you doing this?'

He made a weak gesture with his hands showing the approximate movement made by the dagger throwers, 'Well they wanted to throw ... and the Coliseum won't let them. What could I do?' he said.

'Victor, how much is this costing?'

'Six hundred pounds' he replied.

She could not conceal her sense of outrage, 'How much? *Six hundred pounds*? Are you serious, Victor? Are you mad?'

Like an embarrassed schoolboy, Victor started to shuffle away. 'What could I do?' he kept repeating, 'What could I do?' while his hand continued miming the movement of throwing a dagger. It clearly went against the grain to dispense money on this scale for just one item in the programme but, on the other hand, it was a spectacular showpiece and so he really had no option but to agree to have the stage covered in this way.

The next day was opening night. We became aware that a crowd of protesters was gathering outside both the front and the back of the theatre. A drum beat was followed each time by the unified cry of 'Free Sharansky!' Writer and human rights advocate Anatoly Sharansky's application for an exit visa in order to emigrate to Israel had been refused by the Soviet government on 'security grounds'. His cause had been taken up internationally and the visit by the Georgians provided demonstrators in London with a ready-made opportunity to mount a large-scale protest. (In fact, Sharansky was only able to leave the Soviet Union in 1986 after serving time in the notorious prison camps in very brutal conditions.)

A number of uniformed police were on duty outside the Coliseum. Inside the theatre, we were keyed up, sensing that something was going to happen. However, no additional security staff had been called in by the Coliseum because nobody quite knew the scale of what was about to erupt. The normal theatre staff was deemed to be sufficient to cope, especially as the venue's management thought all the trouble would be outside.

Just as the show was about to start, a dozen women suddenly appeared on the fore-stage, having gained access from the conveniently placed stage boxes where they had been sitting. They all carried umbrellas which concealed their slogan. As they were unfurled, they spelt out a message to free Sharansky. They were ushered off the fore-stage and were escorted from the theatre.

The performance had started when suddenly somebody got up and ran to the front, shouting. Others followed. Every time somebody was escorted out, more trouble started elsewhere in the auditorium. One of my colleagues had been standing with me at the back of the stalls. Now he had become suspicious about somebody he could see who had moved into one of the stage boxes occupied earlier by the umbrella ladies, so he positioned himself in the adjacent box. When the Georgian men started throwing their daggers into the stage, the man leapt from the box and tried to harangue them. Quick as a flash, he was intercepted before he got too far onto the stage and was escorted outside and into the arms of some conveniently waiting policemen. Had he not been stopped, I think it quite likely that he would have suffered an injury from one of the dagger-wielding company who by now were getting very nervous.

The interval came and with it an even greater influx of police, who now positioned themselves inside the auditorium. The second half passed more quietly as most of the demonstrators had already shown their hands. One had even been back at the interval to ask for a refund. At the end of the performance, there was a very large crowd of demonstrators positioned in the narrow street by the stage door. The Metropolitan Police Special Patrol Group had been summoned and a corridor was maintained to allow the performers to get to their coaches for the return journey to the hotel.

The second night we were better prepared but nothing more happened and indeed the rest of the three-week season passed without incident. The Hochhausers, who had been present in the theatre throughout the first performance, were clearly very shaken by the extent of what had happened. By the final week of the run, things were almost back to normal. The Russian ambassador visited and Victor had had a very small quantity of programmes printed with his name on so that he could hand these out to the ambassador and his party.

On the last night, Victor was at the theatre and appeared rather gushing, as if he had had a drink or two. It was a Saturday and he had not driven his car so I gave him and Lillian a lift home. He was unusually animated and started to talk about Anna Barr, or Anna Maximnova as she was better known. She was a pint-sized interpreter who regularly worked for the Hochhausers and I had known her nine years earlier when I was employed by them.

'You know Anna Maximnova,' Victor said. 'When she was a little girl, she sat on Lenin's lap and she's never washed her bottom since then.'

A stunned silence followed broken only by Lillian's cry: 'Victor, how can you say that? How can you say that?'

The following year, Hochhauser booked the Bolshoi Ballet for a six-week season at the Coliseum, although only five weeks were announced initially. He asked me if I could book an orchestra to accompany them and I began organising this. Hochhauser had arranged with the Coliseum that they would manage the season on his behalf so that he could once again keep his name out of the publicity. This time, however, rumours had already started about his involvement. If any proof were needed that he was really behind it, the top ticket price of £12.50 established a new record high for ballet in London and should in itself have been a clear indication of the perpetrator!

The Coliseum's administrator was Rupert Rhymes, later to head the Society of London Theatre. He could be something of a taskmaster and I initially had a slightly strained relationship with him, especially as my colleagues and I nominally had to work through him, whereas all the arrangements for the orchestra had originally been made directly with the Hochhausers. It added what seemed to be an unnecessary layer of administration to work around. However, I subsequently got to know and like Rupert and he was an excellent champion for West End theatre. At the Coliseum, he had a habit of ringing on the internal phone and when somebody answered, shouting a peremptory 'Rupert Rhymes' down the line. He did this one day to the box office manager's extension but the manager was away from his desk and a young Australian newly arrived box office assistant picked up the receiver. 'Rupert Rhymes,' he heard. 'So does duck and f***,' he replied spontaneously, 'but where does that get you?'

Putting together the orchestra was an interesting challenge as the budget was not particularly generous and we wanted to fix a really good band. We were really pleased to book John Georgiadis to lead and I was delighted that the orchestra received a large number of complimentary press notices, sometimes at the expenses of the dancing and the production.

This time, for the first night, the Coliseum was much better prepared than it had been the previous year. There were again demonstrators outside the theatre but a strong line of police kept them from blocking the stage door and the public entrances. Stringent bag searches ensured that nothing sinister was brought into the auditorium and the opening night passed fairly peacefully. Though one evening there was a disturbance when somebody let white mice loose in the auditorium. Much more sinister was the occasion when nails were thrown onto the stage in a deliberate attempt to injure the dancers. I could understand people wanting to protest in a peaceful way but I could never believe that there were those who actually wanted to hurt the performers.

Controversy continued in the press throughout the season with Bernard Levin, the writer and critic, naming Hochhauser as the promoter in an article in *The Times* on the Bolshoi season. The final, sixth week of the season was never announced; I think everyone was glad just to get through the five weeks and go home. After the Bolshoi season, the Hochhausers and the Russians parted company until glasnost and the fall of the Berlin Wall brought about a new era in relations between the East and the West.

My own dealings with the Russians also ended at this point and stayed dormant for the next three years. Then I had a letter from my old friend Klaus Kolmar in New York with whom I had worked with Donald Swann in the 1960s and later with the Tucson Arizona Boys Choir in the UK in 1972 — they were very typical of the boys' choirs in the US and elsewhere, although not so much over here. Dressed in cowboy outfits, they performed a mixed programme from classical to popular hits. Klaus was involved with booking a tour for a Ukrainian folk dance company, Yatran, for an eccentric American entrepreneur whose previous experience had been in the import–export business dealing with the Soviet Union. The Russians had got on well with him – presumably he knew how to play the system – and now, for whatever reason, they wanted him to deal with some of their folk dance ensembles. Klaus wanted to know if I could book some UK dates at the end of their USA tour as it would make good economic sense to stop off in London on the way back to Ukraine.

The promotional material looked promising and I was also happy to take Klaus's word about the quality of the company as he was somebody I knew I could trust. So I fixed up a short tour to tie in with the end of the US dates. I also arranged to go and see the company whilst they were on tour in the

States. However, I suddenly found the city I had booked to visit was no longer correct as the schedule had been changed and they would at that time be playing a four-week season in Philadelphia. Klaus was a bit evasive on the telephone and suggested I stop by in New York to see him on my way to Philadelphia. When we met up, he looked exhausted. He told me the story and it began to dawn on me that we had a potential disaster on our hands.

It seems that the entrepreneur, knowing nothing at all about touring folk dance companies and having been given a schedule with dates which made economic sense with fees and guarantees sufficient to more than cover costs, had nevertheless decided that he wanted things done differently. He had learnt that Philadelphia had the largest Ukrainian émigré population in the whole of the USA and discovered that an infrequently used theatre could be made available to him for four weeks in the middle of the tour. So he had simply cancelled the existing dates and moved the company at relatively short notice into this barn of a theatre into which he had to put everything. He signed a 'four walls' contract with the theatre and that is precisely what he got – a bare stage into which he had to bring settings, lighting, sound and a full stage crew plus front-of-house staff, which in the union-dominated US theatre world added enormously to the costs.

I moved on nervously to Philadelphia in time for the mid-week matinee and found that the theatre was practically empty. When I caught up with the entrepreneur at the end of the performance, he appeared drunk and told me in a slurred voice that we were going to have a huge success in England. I did not like the reference to 'we' as, although he was nominally involved, I had made all the local arrangements and I certainly did not fancy the idea of having him coming over to wreck my plans.

The house was not much better filled for the evening performance and, to make matters worse, I suddenly became aware of an argument going on at the back of the auditorium, behind the curtain which screened the rear lobby. Unable to contain myself, I peeped round only to find the entrepreneur and the tour manager involved in a bout of fisticuffs. The next day, the entrepreneur announced he had himself taken over the duties of the tour manager and, having introduced me to the man from the freight company who would be handling the transfer of the costumes and props to the UK, he again announced that he would be coming with the company.

I flew back in an agitated state. It was clear from what I had seen and from what Klaus Kolmar had told me that it was likely the entrepreneur would go bust before the end of the tour, in which case there was probably no chance of the company coming over for our part. Of course I could not, at short notice, replace the dates with anything else. Apart from the sheer angst and loss of face in having to cancel performances, I would also have faced substantial losses from the bookings I had made for hotels, coaches and of course venues. The insurance I had in place might have mitigated these but it would have been a complicated and uncertain claim.

The first thing I did when I got back was to ascertain that we could block our friend coming over with the company by the simple expedient of not getting him a work permit. I telexed him to explain that it would not be possible for him to accompany the group. Then I contacted Gosconcert in Moscow, again by telex. Gosconcert was the state enterprise that had a monopoly on all Soviet artists, ensembles and companies. They retained a large percentage of the fees paid to individual touring artists, like Oistrakh and Rostropovich, on overseas engagements. In return, they provided a place to live and a certain standard of living back in the Soviet Union but it was by no means an equitable arrangement. The same principle applied to larger groups, with Gosconcert providing all the members with daily living expenses and the local promoter paying for the hotels with breakfast and transport, while Gosconcert pocketed the not insubstantial fees. (This made breakfast a very important meal for Soviet touring companies as they would generally save their 'per diem', or daily stipend, to buy Western goods they could not get at home.) In this case, I'd had no direct dealings with the Soviet authorities, all the arrangements having been made via the USA. I thought it was about time I made a direct approach in order to try to salvage the tour.

I explained in the telex that we had a number of venues all excited and eagerly awaiting the visit by the company but that I was concerned by what was happening in the USA. I received an encouraging but not particularly reassuring response from Moscow. Whilst they were aware of the situation and wished the tour to continue, they said nothing about being able to get the artists to the UK in the event of the US promoter going under.

The final few days before the company was due to arrive were even more tense. They were holed up in a hotel in New York without the means to continue. My position was that we simply did not have the funds available to purchase the air tickets and underwrite other unexpected costs. Our own tour was based on an element of risk and fee paying dates that made sense in its own right. All promoting is undeniably a risk but I was then still a relatively small operator without much financial backing so substantial additional costs would have meant a certain loss for us which we would have been unable to bear, alongside the loss of reputation. I have been close to going under more than once. On one occasion my then accountant advised me to pack it all in and close the business but I am rather glad that I did not do so. Although I have heard it said that you're not a real producer if you haven't come close to the edge, it certainly doesn't feel very good when you are rather near to dropping off it.

It was an anxious time but then finally a call came through from Klaus Kolmar to say that the company would be flying out two days later, arriving during the evening. The night before, I had another call at home saying the plan had changed and they would now be arriving early the very next morning. I managed somehow to get hold of the coach company to alter the pick-up arrangements. I also had to lean on the hotel in order to try to get accommodation ready for the following morning. I made an early dash to Heathrow. The company arrived on an Air India flight looking tired and fed up. They had no money and had eaten very little but at least they were free of that idiot, the American entrepreneur. A hearty English breakfast and a good rest soon had them feeling much better.

Our little tour did very well and the company did an excellent job in presenting themselves to English audiences. Though in Bournemouth, a sad incident marred our joy; two members of the company were arrested for shoplifting. All the memories of Coventry came flooding back but this time there was no relatively happy ending as both were charged and subsequently fined. Fortunately, we managed to keep it out of the papers.

Gosconcert sent one of their senior people from Moscow to see the company on tour and so I was able to start a direct dialogue with them. A few months later, in 1978, my wife and I were invited to Moscow. We arrived at Sheremetyevo airport on a very cold January day and were met by Henrietta, our interpreter and guide. I had never been to Moscow before and it was exciting to visit so many of the places which I only knew by name. We stayed at the Metropol Hotel in a charming room full of antiques. From the window, we could see the Bolshoi Theatre. The restaurant offered an enormous selection of delicacies but the problem was that virtually none of them were available. It seemed that the hotel liked to give the impression that it had a fantastic cuisine, and maybe once it had, but shortages meant that the actual choice was very limited. Getting somebody to take the order was the first hurdle, even before the lengthy business of first selecting dishes and then finding out that none were available. In the end, I always found it simpler to ask what we could have and with luck there might be a choice of three or four dishes.

Entry to the hotel was controlled by a doorman who always demanded to see the hotel pass. Each floor was controlled by a *babushka*, normally humourless and sitting strategically at a desk close to the elevator, noting down all the comings and goings. However, I never experienced what my father heard from one of his clients who had accompanied Harold Macmillan as one of the press corps to Moscow in 1959. Then, aware that their rooms were almost certainly bugged, they would turn on the radio quite loudly only to find it decreasing in volume seemingly of its own volition. So they decided one day to complain to each other that there were never any fresh eggs available for breakfast. The following morning, much to their delight, a basket of freshly boiled eggs had been set out for them on the breakfast table.

After a couple of days in Moscow, we were taken to see various companies in Kiev including the local Red Army Ensemble. Normally, we were given private performances followed by a lot of eating, drinking toasts and endless enquiries as to how much we had enjoyed the performance, not least because all these companies dreamt of going on tour in the West where they would have access to Western goods. However, on this occasion, the Red Army performance was not private, it was a normal public performance and, as we discovered, had not been filleted for visiting Western tastes. Here we really did get to see a number called 'Down on the Collective Farm', showing jolly Ukrainian country boys and girls enjoying tractor driving and gathering the harvest. More was to follow; there was a compere who introduced the programme and added what appeared to be political comments from time to time, although with my very limited Russian I could understand none of this and Henrietta, the interpreter, stopped translating at these times, always a sign of something untoward. At the end of the first half, the compere's attitude changed and he became much more of a rabble-rouser, launching into a diatribe which included frequent references to the 'Americansky'. We did not really need a translation; it was clearly a tirade aimed against the West and Henrietta looked quite embarrassed as the house lights came up. 'You don't want to stay for the second half, do you?' she asked sheepishly. 'Not really,' I replied.

Back in Moscow, I signed a protocol covering proposed visits by the Georgian State Dance Company and the Violins of the Bolshoi, a string group drawn from the Bolshoi orchestra with solo singers from the Bolshoi itself. I was quite pleased with this result and we went through another round of toasts to eternal friendship before leaving for the airport. The lengthy check-in and security checks – more at that time to do with whether you were genuinely the person detailed in the passport and whether you were removing anything from the Soviet Union that you should not rather than concerns about flight safety – produced its own tensions. When the plane had been airborne for a good hour, the pilot announced that we had just left Soviet airspace. There was a spontaneous burst of applause from the delighted passengers. It was just like being let out of school.

The visit by the Georgians in 1979 was a far cry from their visit six years earlier when the London Coliseum had exploded with protestors on the opening night. Gosconcert had not given me a lot of time to arrange the visit and it had been impossible to find a central London venue with sufficient dates available for a ten-day run so I placed them instead at Wembley. The newly opened conference centre adjoined the arena and had a good-sized auditorium with modern facilities but it was not the same as playing right in the heart of town. It has since been demolished but features in an often-repeated episode of the late seventies ITV series *The Professionals*, so it's not entirely forgotten. The tour on the whole went well with little sign of the demonstrations that so affected the previous tour.

At Manchester, I had pencilled in three dates at the Palace Theatre but the theatre refused to confirm the booking, insisting that I must hire the venue rather than go ahead on the usual sharing terms, an arrangement whereby the box office proceeds are divided in some agreed ratio between the producer and the venue. This was contrary to what we had earlier discussed and the dates were important to me as they were right in the middle of the tour. I certainly did not want to underwrite the cost of hiring the theatre as well as paying all the company's costs so I embarked on a high-risk strategy to break the deadlock. I prepared a telex in the name of Novosti Press in London, the official Soviet news agency, which was addressed to the *Manchester Evening News*. When I say 'prepared' I mean just that – this was the time of the old-style telex machines where one had to punch out a tape and the series of holes created ensured that the message was typed out correctly at the other end. The tape was then fed through the telex machine once contact had been made with the other side. The message I sent stated that Gosconcert had decided to withdraw all Soviet artists from future performances in Manchester as a result of the theatre's refusal to confirm the booking of the Georgians. The ruse worked; within thirty minutes, the director of the theatre was on the line. As I had hoped, the newspaper had called him for a quote. 'This is all a misunderstanding,' he said. 'Of course we want to take the Georgians and on sharing terms too.' Thank goodness nobody ever discovered what I had done.

Over the next three years, I brought over several Soviet groups besides the Georgians but the market was changing and the audiences for this type of thing were slipping. One of my last visits to the Soviet Union was to visit Lvov in western Ukraine in order to see the Virsky Company. Lvov itself was a very interesting city which had not been a part of Ukraine for very long. Up until the end of the First World War it had been known as Lemberg, part of the old Austro-Hungarian Empire in an area known as Galicia. It had been joined to post-First World War Poland and was the scene of terrible atrocities during the German occupation in the Second World War.

The guide who had been assigned to show us round took us through the town, pointing out some historical places of interest from the old Hapsburg days before driving up a hillside to a point overlooking the town so that we could get a good panoramic view. As we gazed down, he went through a brief history ending with the fact that at the outbreak of the Second World War, the citizens called upon their brother Ukrainians in the Soviet Union to help them in their hour of need and thus Polish Lviv became Soviet Lvov. 'Well,' he ended, with a twinkle in his eye, 'that's our story and we intend to stick with it; I know you learn something different in the West.' I was struck by the sense of both humour and candour in his remark. It was rare to find somebody prepared to be honest when talking to Westerners in what was then still the period of the Cold War.

During the same visit, I was staying in Moscow and going to see the final of the Tchaikovsky Competition at the Moscow Conservatoire. Originally for violin and piano participants, this prestigious international competition was started in 1958 and held every four years, alternating between Moscow and Saint Petersburg (or Leningrad, as it was then still called). My interpreter, Nina, had already told me an interesting story about our previous interpreter, Henrietta, who I knew had been married to a Spaniard who had fled to Russia at the end of the Spanish Civil War. Nina believed that he was actually Trotsky's assassin, Ramon Mercader. Whether or not Henrietta was really Mrs Mercader I never discovered, although the other part of the story, that she was a decorated colonel in the KGB, seemed to be correct from everything that I was able to learn about her.

As it was a fine day, Nina suggested we walk back to the hotel and we went through back streets towards the Metropol. We passed an old church, of which there are many such to be seen in Moscow, but this one was different in that it was open. I had forgotten it was Sunday and a service was in progress. Nina asked if I would like to go inside and then she spoke to one of the militiamen on duty outside who let us pass. Inside, the church was packed, with many people having to stand. There was an intensity about the religious service which was deeply moving. The congregation seemed to consist entirely of elderly people, most of them women. We did not stay long; I felt we were intruding on something rather private and very special. As we left, I thought how extraordinary it was that in spite of all the efforts of a brutalist regime to stamp out religion, the light of faith still burnt as brightly as ever. Since glasnost and perestroika, all this has changed but, at the time, it was deeply, deeply moving.

My final dealings with the Soviets concerned the Red Army Ensemble. I had booked an eight-week tour for the spring of 1980 which included a week at the Royal Albert Hall. All the arrangements were in place and if the interest from the venues was anything to go by, it looked already as if it was going to be a great success. As usual with major events, I had insured it for all risks. Just at the moment when we were starting to prepare publicity material, there was a nasty surprise. The Red Army had decided to invade Afghanistan and so one might imagine the Red Army Ensemble appearing in downtown Kabul rather than at the Royal Albert Hall.

The invasion caused considerable outrage and some of the venues which were council-owned wanted to cancel dates. I was in a very difficult position. I too wanted to cancel as it was not the moment to be bringing Russian soldiers into the UK, even comic ones who sang and danced, but I could not act alone. My insurance would not cover me if I myself cancelled the tour. The other side had to do it and it was clear that Gosconcert would not oblige. They felt it would damage the prestige of the Soviet Union if they were seen to back down and cancel the tour in the face of Western threats.

Questions were asked in Parliament and pieces started to appear in the press. My local MP, Sydney Chapman, was extremely helpful and I also had contacts at the Foreign Office through my earlier dealings with the Russians whom I now asked for help. I received a summons to see the Foreign Office Minister, Richard Luce. I explained my predicament to him; he was sympathetic but could promise nothing. I was beginning to understand diplomatic niceties and I took this as meaning, 'Hang on, we are doing what we can.' So I came away from the meeting feeling mildly encouraged. Then the British Government informed the Soviet authorities that a tour by the Red Army would not be helpful in the present circumstances, diplomatic parlance for 'cancel or else'. The Russians felt that as this represented an official threat, they could use it as an appropriate excuse to withdraw from the tour. A telex arrived from Gosconcert confirming the cancellation.

Now I had to make the insurance claim. There was an all-embracing war clause in the policy which might affect the validity of our claim. I took expert advice and stood firm. A loss adjuster was appointed. Eventually, we received an offer of £60,000 in settlement. It was slightly below what I was anticipating but I readily accepted it. Except that the loss adjuster tried one last trick and asked me to go and see him. If I was prepared to accept £60,000, he said, why would I not take, say, £50,000. I walked out of his office without saying anything, leaving him open-mouthed and speechless. A few days later the cheque arrived.

CHAPTER EIGHT

VIENNA, CITY OF DREAMS

One of my earliest shows, a programme of Viennese music performed by three singers and a pianist, was given in hundreds of performances around the country when I was just starting out in my business. Later, I had been able to add a small orchestra for dates in the larger venues and so, when I started working at the Queen Elizabeth Hall on the South Bank and later the Royal Festival Hall, it was natural for me to schedule these Viennese programmes from time to time. In 1972, Associated Television had presented a lavish eight-part drama series, *The Strauss Family*, on prime-time television with music provided by the London Symphony Orchestra. It seems virtually impossible to imagine commercial television these days investing in a full series of this kind, telling the story of Johann Strauss the Elder and his three sons, including Johann II, the waltz king. But then it did much to increase the popularity of the music.

I was aware that 1975 was the 150th anniversary of the birth of Johann Strauss and, as the South Bank had allocated three dates over the May bank holiday weekend to me, I decided to use these to give a series of three concerts marking the anniversary. The first two would be straightforward orchestral concerts featuring different aspects of the Strauss family's works but the third would be a little different. I wanted to capture some of the glamour and romance of the television series and so decided to incorporate dancers alongside a small orchestra.

I had no idea how to go about booking a group of dancers so I turned to the wife of one of the singers with whom I had regularly worked since I started on my own, as she was a dancer. She said she would be able to book a suitable number from the freelance circuit and that she would also be able

....
87

to choreograph the various dance items in the programme. It struck me that the cost and effort in doing all this for just one performance was not going to be worthwhile so I arranged a three-week series of dates at halls around the country to tie in with the QEH, starting with three performances at Eastbourne where, at the time, I was doing a lot of work at the Congress Theatre.

I needed to find a conductor who could direct the orchestra from the violin in the same way that the Strauss father and son had done and I asked John Georgiadis whether he might be interested. He had been the youngest leader ever of the City of Birmingham Symphony Orchestra and later leader of the LSO. I had worked with him and his then wife, Sue, a viola player who sometimes accompanied him, including presenting them together in a duo evening at the QEH. Our singer was Marilyn Hill Smith, then married to Peter Kemp of the Johann Strauss Society, which was very useful in helping find suitable programme ideas.

John Georgiadis took to the whole Strauss idea with gusto and the tour proved a huge success, so much so that I immediately booked an autumn tour and started making plans for three tours the following year. The choreography was the only thing which I felt needed looking at but I was fortunate in being able to interest Geraldine Stephenson in the idea. It was she who had done all the choreography for the television series and she had expert knowledge and really interesting ideas for staging the dances. I worked happily with her for many years.

By the autumn of 1976, I was presenting about sixty performances a year of the *Johann Strauss Gala* including a couple at the Royal Albert Hall. Just after the start of this autumn tour, I began to get one or two calls from various venues saying that John Georgiadis had approached them saying that he was sure they would want to deal with him directly when he did his own Johann Strauss tours starting the following year. I was sent copies of the letters he was handing out giving details of his plans. Of course, he did not talk to me about this and had been doing it covertly whilst still directing the dates on my tour.

I decided that this was rather too serious a matter for me to tackle face to face so I hurried over to my solicitor for advice. He talked me through the options, the best of which seemed to be to go for an injunction. We went to see counsel – all this was very new to me and deeply worrying. An injunction was fine, if it could be obtained, but it carried with it awesome responsibilities in the event that Georgiadis subsequently fought it and won. On the other hand, all the professional advice indicated that I had a very strong case. If granted, an injunction would force the other party to cease in his efforts to wrest the business from me.

One Friday in early October, I found myself alongside Tony Gee, my solicitor, the only spectators in a judge's chambers, whilst our counsel argued our case. I had been up half the night preparing a series of exhibits for the court which counsel had asked for. These had to be numbered and listed in a special way. By the time I was in court, I was tired and fractious. Our barrister put the case very well and I started to feel slightly more optimistic when the judge saw a copy of the newspaper advertisement listing the tour dates and remarked that, yes, he had seen these in the national papers. At the end, he announced he was minded to grant an ex-parte injunction preventing Georgiadis from contacting the venues. This meant that he would have to stop immediately in his efforts to solicit dates from the venues I was using. My solicitor and I hurried round to the stamping room to get a copy of the order stamped up and ready for immediate issue.

The show that night was at Tunbridge Wells. We arrived for the last half hour or so of the performance. I felt unusually nervous as we stood at the back of the auditorium waiting for it to finish. As soon as the last bars of the final encore faded and the applause started, we went backstage to John Georgiadis' dressing room. I introduced him to my solicitor, who said, 'Sorry, but this is an order from the court preventing you from soliciting or otherwise interfering with the bookings for the *Johann Strauss Gala*.' He added for good measure that Georgiadis was sacked from the rest of the tour, which still had another four weeks to run. John Georgiadis ran from the room shouting, 'Look what they've done to me.' That was the last I saw of him for five years.

Even before I knew what John Georgiadis had been doing, I was aware that he was unlikely to want to commit to further tours so I had already approached Jack Rothstein, another fine leader and soloist, to see if he might be interested in taking over. He had even been to see the show at the Royal Albert Hall at the start of the present tour. A couple of days before I sacked Georgiadis, I approached him in great secrecy to see whether he could take over any of the present tour. He could, he said, but not immediately, which left me with an awkward eight-day period to cover immediately after Tunbridge Wells. Marcus Dods, dear Marcus, who had always been so supportive and who was musical director of my London Concert Orchestra, agreed to conduct from the baton for the eight-day period and so we were safe.

The next day, I had to announce to a startled orchestra that Georgiadis would not be appearing with them again. The crisis was over but it had taught me a very firm lesson in how to deal with such situations. I could have taken the easy option, rolled over and let Georgiadis have his way. I chose instead to take a firm if risky line and issued a writ; I won.

Some weeks later, I was told about a session, one of those commercial recordings beloved of freelance musicians made up on the day with leaders and senior players from many orchestras all attracted by the good fees on offer. Georgiadis was there and by this time it was pretty common knowledge around the session world that I had issued a writ and obtained an injunction against him. So when the conductor announced, 'Let's make a *rit* here,' (a *ritardando* or gradual slowing down) all the other string players, hearing 'rit' and thinking of 'writ', turned to John, pointing their bows and said, 'Aha ... '

There is an ultimate happy ending to this story. At the rehearsal for my very first Barbican concert in April 1982, the LSO asked if they might bring in Maestro Celibidache to listen to the hall's acoustics. He came surrounded by several acolytes, including John Georgiadis, by now back as leader of the LSO. We shook hands and old enmities were forgotten. Since then, I have worked happily with him on many occasions.

The success of the Strauss gala led me to think about other Viennese attractions. For years, the New Year's Day concert from Vienna had been a regular fixture on the BBC and, even as a youngster, I remembered seeing the smiling face of Willi Boskovsky directing the Vienna Philharmonic through a programme of Strauss family music. So I wrote to him in Vienna and asked whether he might be interested in conducting the London Concert Orchestra in a series of half a dozen concerts at the Royal Festival Hall and around the country. I do not suppose he had ever heard of the London Concert Orchestra but I had by happy chance got to him at a highly appropriate time. He had been doing regular concerts with the BBC Concert Orchestra but there had been a falling out and he had no immediate plans to be in England. So, when my invitation came, he decided he would accept.

I met him some weeks later at Lacy's, a rather nice restaurant just off Tottenham Court Road round the corner from my office. He spent a great deal of the time we had together talking about himself, how he was the best known person in Vienna, how he had been voted number one personality in Norway (yes, really) and so on, and I nodded agreeably throughout this one-man litany. Eventually, we got down to brass tacks, fixed the fee, which was seemingly very high, tackled the expenses, which was really very simple – I would pay all of them – and talked over the rehearsal and performance schedule. The tour was not for another nine months so we had good time to put everything in place. I had lined up a good orchestra with no deputies allowed. The practice of players being able to substitute others in their place if a more lucrative engagement comes up is one that is always difficult for foreign conductors to understand and I was determined not to allow it. I was helped by having by now seven concerts and three paid rehearsals which meant the players would be earning good money for the ten-day period involved.

I met Willi at the airport the day before the first rehearsal. His wife was not with him as anticipated. 'She has a cold,' he said. 'She will come later.' Willi and colds, I discovered, did not mix. At the initial rehearsal, Bridget, who sat on the first desk of second violins, right under the conductor's nose, had had a nosebleed in the break. She came back clutching a handkerchief to her face. 'Go to the back,' ordered Willi. It was no good arguing with him, his Teutonic authority would not brook any discussion. 'When you have a cold, you go to the back,' he announced to the full orchestra before resuming the rehearsal.

The rehearsals were very enjoyable for the players even though Willi was very demanding. He had the authentic style which brought to life the Viennese lilt of the waltzes, polkas and marches. The players were learning something from him; it was certainly no routine play through of a dozen hackneyed Strauss pieces. Here was a march by Suppé from *Fatinitza*, which I doubt any of them had played before; here were Strauss rarities and novelty pieces mixed with some of the better-known favourites.

Willi had a penchant for staying at the Holiday Inn in Swiss Cottage. 'I can walk to Rossetti's [a well-known nearby pub] for a beer,' he said. How he had discovered the hotel in the first place, I never found out. For the first concert, at Slough, I arranged to pick him up and drive him there. The concert itself went very well with a packed house and an appreciative audience, which was just as well as he was determined, come what may, to play at least four encores.

Under the terms of our agreement, I was obliged to pay him in Swiss francs at the conclusion of each concert. We had originally negotiated in pounds but the continuing fall of the pound sterling, especially against the Swiss franc, had frightened him to the extent that he insisted on changing this. Back at the hotel, he invited me in for a beer and I handed over his money, which he counted twice, very carefully. The same thing happened the next day after our concert at St Albans, except this time, after he had counted the money, he said, 'You know, I trust you; you can from now on pay me after every second concert.' This, I felt, was meant as a great accolade.

During this first tour, the former prime minister Edward Heath decided at the last minute that he wanted to come to the Royal Festival Hall and I found myself trying to find seats for him in an otherwise sold-out performance. I ended up giving him the box I was keeping for my own use. Heath had invited Willi to lunch at his London house the following Sunday and so I arranged to pick Willi up from there and drive him to Bournemouth for our concert that evening. Heath emerged from his house and asked if I would like to join the remainder of the party for coffee but I declined — I felt that if I was going to be treated as the chauffeur, I might as well play the role to the full and stay by the car.

By this time, Willi's wife, Elisabeth, had arrived and we started referring to her, out of earshot, as Mrs Willi. She had been an actress and was some years younger than her husband. She happily devoted herself to supporting him and accompanied him to every concert. She had a habit of repeating what he said so it became a kind of echo. Once, on the second tour at

Brighton, he got very angry because seats behind the orchestra had not been sold through lack of demand. Normally, when there were people sitting behind he could only smile at the orchestra, but this time he snarled at them like an angry lion about to pounce on anyone who even hinted at a hurried tempo or a cracked note.

In the interval, in his dressing room, he announced that he was not happy. 'He is not happy,' added Mrs Willi.

'You have the Royal Festival Hall tomorrow,' he announced, as if somehow I was not aware of this. Mrs Willi repeated this. 'I will be ill,' he said.

'Yes, he will be ill,' she added.

Nonchalantly, I nodded. 'OK,' I said, 'call me in the morning and if you cannot go on, I'll get somebody else.'

What was I saying? How could I possibly replace Willi and at a moment's notice? The bluff worked though — by the end of the show he had snapped back to normal, aided by enthusiastic applause and the long line of mostly elderly women seeking his autograph backstage. Not a lot was said on the drive back to London but as I dropped them off at the hotel he smiled and said, 'See you tomorrow.' To which I happily replied, 'Yes, of course.'

Willi's biography in the programme was very comprehensive but there was one rather obvious gap in it. After detailing how he had become the youngest ever leader of the Vienna Philharmonic in 1933, it went straight on to reveal what he was doing after 1945. I never did discover what he did during the war although I believe it was a very sensitive subject for him.

Once, during the time he was working with the BBC, he overheard the first desk of violins using the dreaded 'N word' when talking about his wartime activities during a break in the rehearsal. He moved across seemingly to look at the pad of the players on the desk behind and very deliberately and carefully put his foot down on the leader's pipe which had been lying alongside his fiddle case on the floor. It snapped in two. 'Oh,' said Willi, 'I'm so sorry.'

On the other hand, when I was driving him one day to Birmingham, he looked across as we skirted a largish town whose outline was visible from the motorway. 'What is that place?' he enquired.

'That's Coventry,' I replied.

'Ah,' he said, 'it was terribly destroyed in the war.'

The drives with him were always interesting, even when, one day, on the way to Reading through the Friday afternoon rush-hour traffic, he regaled me with his story of waking up at the hotel in the morning and turning on the radio. 'They were playing the Spohr Octet; it was marvellous and I wondered who could be playing the violin so beautifully. Then it ended and they announced the artists and, you know what, it was me playing,' he said, without the hint of a smile.

Fortunately, I did not drive him and Elisabeth down to Eastbourne later that week. When they arrived, the first thing they told me with great excitement was that on the journey they had passed eighty-seven sets of traffic lights. 'And do you know that fifty-three were red and thirty-four were green?'

This was during his second tour for me, which I had negotiated at the conclusion of the previous year's very successful initial tour. He had decided to change some of the programme for the second concert at the Royal Festival Hall, which followed a week after the first. So, at the last concert before the return to the Festival Hall, which happened to be at Wembley, he was determined to play through all the new items as encores even though they had already been meticulously rehearsed. The applause at the end of the official programme was good, the sort of level that would normally guarantee him two encores. He managed to play seven. The section of the audiences that was tiring and wanting to go home was counterbalanced by those who were fascinated to see the maestro return to the podium after taking a quick bow between each number and raise his baton for yet one more encore. It was that kind of curiosity where they felt they had to keep up the applause just to see how far he would go. Once he had finished number seven, he hopped offstage with a self-satisfied look saying as he brushed past me, 'Now we have rehearsed everything for tomorrow.'

Willi was due to make a third tour in 1979 but was forced to cancel very late on after he was diagnosed with a serious heart condition. Henry Krips stepped in at the last minute and saved the day. Although he was an excellent conductor and handled the style beautifully, it was never quite the same as Willi who brought a certain magic to the concerts. In the early 1980s, Willi came back one more time for me but the concerts were a shadow of what they had once been; he seemed to have lost the vigour and drive which so contributed to his earlier success and the audiences too had drifted away. Willi no longer conducted the New Year's Day concert and his popularity, it seemed, had waned with this. His many recordings, not just of the popular Viennese repertoire, live on as a testimony to his graceful and dignified style and above all his sense of charm and romance. I was always glad that I had the chance to work with him.

At home in Golders Green, circa 1950.
Mum, Dad and my brother Nicholas
are playing proper instruments while
I'm just blowing my own (toy) trumpet.

PALACE PIER THEATRE
BRIGHTON — Telephone 682276

SUNDAY CONCERTS! at 8 pm
By arrangement with Miles Byrne
RAYMOND GUBBAY presents

2nd JULY
MARION STUDHOLME
(Covent Garden/Sadler's Wells) IN
VIENNESE EVENING
with Alan Morrell tenor Robert Bateman baritone John Parry piano
Popular items from the great Viennese Operettas, including Die Fledermaus, The Merry Widow
The Count of Luxemburg, The Gipsy Baron, The Chocolate Soldier, The Gipsy Princess

30th JULY
JOHN HEDDLE NASH
(Sadler's Wells, Radio & Television) IN
An evening of GILBERT & SULLIVAN
with Robin Bell soprano Julia Meadows mezzo-soprano
Edmund Bohan tenor Mary Hill piano
Excerpts from the Savoy Operas, including The Mikado, Iolanthe, The Yeomen of the Guard
The Gondoliers, H.M.S. Pinafore, The Pirates of Penzance, Ruddigore, Utopia Limited

27th AUGUST
JOHN HEDDLE NASH
(Sadler's Wells, Radio & Television) IN
SONGS FROM THE SHOWS
with Robin Bell soprano Edmund Bohan tenor Mary Hill piano
Songs from the great Musical Shows, including items from the works of Ivor Novello
Sigmund Romberg, Rogers and Hammerstein, Friml, etc.

Tickets (All bookable in advance): 10/- 7/6 5/- Boxes for 3, 30/- Boxes for 2, 20/-

Left: *Flyer for my three Sunday concerts at the Palace Pier, Brighton, 1967. I used to help out in the box office, selling tickets on the day.*

Right: *The box office return for the very first concerts I ever put on, at the wonderful Theatre Royal, Bury St Edmunds, October 1966, all in old pounds, shillings and pence.*

Below: *My first national press review in* The Times, *1971. It still reads quite well despite the misspelling of D'Oyly Carte. I like the reference to 'the young impresario'!*

G and S centenary concert

Queen Elizabeth Hall

Alan Blyth

When *Thespis* was given at the Gaiety Theatre in London on December 26 a hundred years ago the Gilbert and Sullivan partnership was born. To celebrate the occasion, the young impresario Raymond Gubbay had the idea of brightening a rather dull Sunday with a centenary concert in the Queen Elizabeth Hall. He was naturally rewarded with a full house. He and Marcus Dodds, the evening's conductor, had also turned up a couple of numbers from the lost unpublished score, which nobody in 1871 guessed would be the start of something so auspicious.

One of these, "Climbing over rocky mountains", was later used in *The Pirates of Penzance* so that only the words, unintelligible in an ensemble, were "new". The other piece, "Little Mary of Arcady" has apparently been available as a song with piano. It has now been orchestrated by Dodds. Perhaps it is not a ditty immediately to identify Sullivan as the future composer of so many singable tunes or Gilbert as the caustic wit he was to become, but it is disarmingly catchy. Leslie Randall, who introduced the items at rather too great a length, pointed out that at the bottom of the libretto's cover are the words in small print. "original music by Arthur Sullivan".

For the rest, the fare was familiar—highlights, you might say with the record companies, from the regular Savoy Opera's repertory served up with the emphasis on the music. Mr Dodds and the New Promenade Orchestra began each section with one of the overtures, as if to let us savour for once Sullivan's keen ear for orchestral colour even when his harmony is inevitably conservative.

Marion Studholme, who is happily down for some Blondes at the Coliseum soon, was a purer, surer, more agile singer of the soprano roles than you are ever likely to come across in the D'Oyley Carte company. Her accounts of "The sun whose rays" and "Poor wandering one"—the latter with a boldly executed cadenza—were perhaps worthy of a more discerning public.

Jean Temperley has not quite the commanding low notes for G and S's heavy contralto roles, but then who has these days? Her diction was impeccable; so was that of John Heddle Nash who delivered the patter songs with panache, every word cleanly inflected. He allowed himself some harmless verbal licence in "As some day it may happen". Edmund Bohan's light, lyrical tenor had good, old-fashioned vocal manners, spoilt only by effortful high notes.

Above: *My sales pitch for the 1970/71 season. I sent out this brochure to halls and theatres around the country. My life then was endless touring and I loved it.*

Below: *In my dickie bow, all of eighteen years old, in 1965. The Red Navy Choir was finishing a ten-week tour in Blackpool and I managed to get them to pose for this souvenir photo.*

From top: *With Pavarotti at the Barbican, 1985. He was so kind and obliging – it was a real pleasure to work with him.*

With Aled Jones and composer Howard Blake backstage at the Barbican in 1985. Aled had the most glorious boy soprano voice, strong and beautifully focused.

I worked many times with Yehudi Menuhin at the Barbican. Here we are backstage in 1986 with soloist Eduard Wulfson and violin dealer Peter Biddulph on the left and his wife.

From top: *I put together an evening of the music of Andrew Lloyd Webber which toured in 1987 with Sarah Brightman and Michael Ball as the vocal stars. This was taken at Birmingham's NEC.*

After recording Desert Island Discs *with Kirsty Young in 2006. It was such an enjoyable morning, even though she asked some tough questions!*

In the Royal Retiring Room at the Royal Albert Hall with Mrs T during the run of Tosca *in 2009. We talked about her win in Finchley in 1958 when I was a schoolboy living close by in Golders Green.*

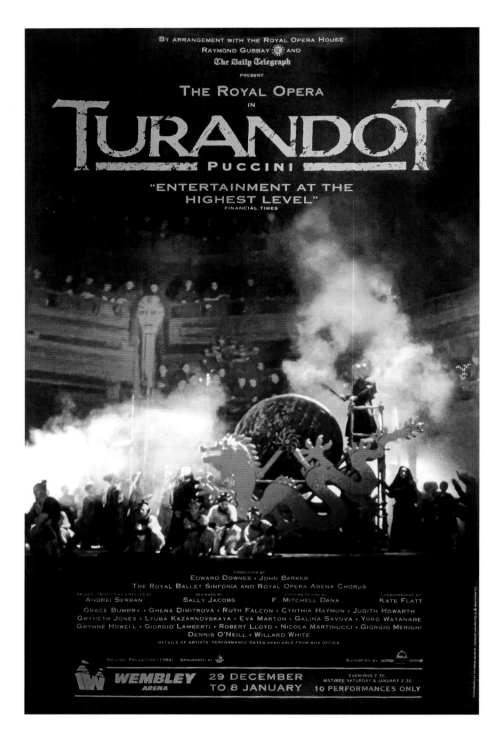

Above: *The poster for* Turandot *with the Royal Opera House at Wembley in 1991/92. Ten performances with five different Turandots and six different Calafs. I watched every performance.*

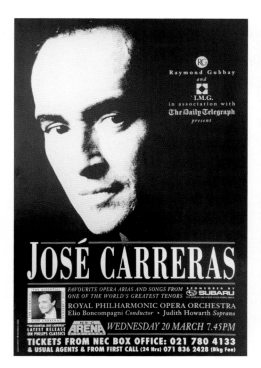

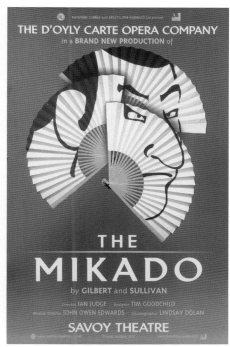

*A small selection of posters for some of the wonderful performances I have been involved in over the years:
José Carreras, 1989; The Mikado, 2000; Itzhak Perlman, 1995; Madam Butterfly, 1998.*

Above: *Respectability at last! Receiving my honorary fellowship from Trinity College of Music, London, in 2001. Sir Cameron Mackintosh is on the left, Sir John Tooley is next to me and Gavin Henderson, principal at the time, is in the second row.*

Below: *2001. 'Music, Ma'am!' shouted the equerry as I moved forward. 'Oh, you are in music,' said Her Majesty.*

CHAPTER NINE

THE BARBICAN OPENS

The historic area between Moorgate and Aldersgate in the City of London suffered extensive bomb damage in December 1941 during the height of the Blitz. The narrow streets and ancient buildings that housed a mixture of artisans and merchants were almost completely destroyed. The Germans had carefully chosen a time when the Thames was at its lowest so that it was difficult to pump water from the river. At one point, fire appliances had been called to London from as far afield as Norfolk and Birmingham to help fight the fires, so great was the extent of the blaze.

Miraculously, St Paul's Cathedral escaped largely undamaged thanks partly to the brave fire watchers who even pushed incendiary devices off the roof in some cases with nothing more than broom handles. When a British Movietone News cameraman arrived at St Paul's at the height of the Blitz, he was not allowed to go up to the roof as it was considered too dangerous. When he argued with the verger, saying it was history which needed to be recorded, the verger relented but he still charged him sixpence (2.5 pence), the normal cost of a ticket for going up to the dome. The footage he took that day has become some of the most iconic images of the Blitz.

However, away from St Paul's, where once Hepplewhite had had his workshop and the Worcester Porcelain Company its London repository, and where Hester Bateman, the famous Georgian silversmith had worked, lay only rubble and dirt. After the war, the Corporation of the City of London resolved to rebuild the area and to provide modern housing. Somewhere along the line, they decided to provide a new home for the Guildhall School of Music and Drama, then housed in cramped conditions in John Carpenter Street. Later still, the plans were altered so that the small concert hall and adjoining theatre could be enlarged and offered as permanent homes to the London Symphony Orchestra and the Royal Shakespeare Company. By 1970, they had even appointed a director for the arts complex. Henry Wrong was a Canadian whose early career had included spells working for the Metropolitan Opera in New York and the newly constructed National Arts Center in Ottawa.

Henry Wrong eventually waited twelve years from his appointment in 1970 until the centre opened in 1982. Several times, the City Corporation voted on whether to abandon the project and the opening date was constantly being put back. However, by 1979 it looked as though the centre would be opening two years later and so I wrote to Henry to introduce myself and to express an interest in promoting concerts in the new concert hall. My first visit to the Barbican followed a few weeks later when I met Henry for the first time. He was a tall, debonair character, outwardly ebullient but, as I later learnt, privately quite waspish and always immaculately turned out in a well-cut suit.

Henry gave me boots and a hard hat to wear and we made our way into the centre. Although it was unfinished, all the main features were in place with the roof on and so it was possible to visit every part of the building and to begin to imagine how it would look when it was fully fitted out. The sheer size and scale of the project made a deep and immediate impression on me and I realised at once that nothing on this scale was ever likely to be built again in London in my lifetime. So I resolved on the spot to take dates there.

The planned opening for 1981 was later put back a year but the centre now began to take on a full complement of staff to plan and to market the complex. The new opening date was set for 3 March 1982 and I reserved a few dates in April and May to follow the opening concert season by the London Symphony Orchestra.

In February, tickets for the April dates went on sale. I had three concerts planned for the Easter weekend, 10 to 12 April 1982 — dates I well remember. An opera gala with Josephine Barstow on Saturday; an all-Beethoven programme with pianist Cristina Ortiz and the Royal Philharmonic Orchestra conducted by Norman Del Mar on Sunday and the Johann Strauss Gala on Easter Monday.

A few days after the tickets had gone on sale, I telephoned the box office for the sales reports; the initial figures were not bad but neither were they overly encouraging. Two days later, I rang again for an update and discovered that the figures had shot up. So I called the box office manager to make sure there had not been a mistake. No, not at all, he said, it was just that they had been overwhelmed by the amount of postal bookings and it was taking them some time to process all of these. Within a few days, all three concerts had sold out and I found myself having to schedule extra performances – and all of this before the centre had actually opened. This showed me for the first time that the Barbican was going to be a success, at least for my type of concert. A golden sunrise has suddenly appeared over a wintry London where, unbeknown to a wider public at this stage, the country was heading towards the Falklands War.

The box office was run by Peter Skinner who, together with his sister and deputy, Eileen Tench, had moved across from the Aldwych Theatre where they had run the box office for the Royal Shakespeare Theatre. Peter and Eileen, together with their team of former colleagues from the Aldwych and an influx of keen recruits, faced a formidable challenge as the Barbican had installed a computer box office system, one of the earliest in a major venue. To say they rose to the challenge is an understatement. They and their enthusiastic team very quickly adapted to the new way of working and there were very few glitches along the way. Among their new recruits was Karl Sydow, who had previously worked in a bookshop. He took to computers like a duck to water, soon becoming the resident expert with the Barbican's system, as well as a good and helpful friend to me during those early days at the centre. He went on to greater glory, initially with the development of box office computer systems and then as a highly successful theatre producer.

My wife and I were invited to the opening along with virtually the entire arts and entertainment's establishment and a vast contingent from the City. The Queen sat for half the evening in the concert hall and the other half in the theatre. At the conclusion, there was a wonderful spread of food and drink laid out in the various foyers but with warning notices proclaiming 'Please do not start to eat until after the Queen has departed' which caused merriment amongst some of the theatrical luvvies who were present.

It later transpired that immediately prior to the Queen's arrival, one unfortunate guest had suffered a fatal heart-attack but there was no time to remove the body, which was lying very close to where the Queen would shortly be passing. With considerable presence of mind, one of the senior Barbican officials gathered up some of the nearby floral decorations and placed them on the corpse just before the Queen appeared. The body was tactfully removed after the start of the overture.

The interest in the opening had been enormous with press and television reports carried around the world. I suppose the project had been so long in coming to fruition that much of the interest stemmed from sheer amazement that it was actually finished. The final bill of £156 million was another cause for astonishment as it was way over budget and was, at the time, the most expensive arts complex ever built.

My relationship with the centre blossomed almost immediately. I suddenly found myself with sold-out concerts and offers to take on more and more dates. The symphony concerts that I organised seemed to sell out quickly and there were often queues waiting for return tickets. This was at a time when the rest of the concert world was suffering badly from the effects of the Falklands War and a general economic downturn. The Argentinian Ambassador had tried unsuccessfully to cancel his subscription to the London Symphony Orchestra; he was recalled home without a refund.

In the first year, I promoted over fifty concerts with an average attendance of over ninety per cent. The Barbican was clearly working for me and working well. It had become my lode stone, a new venue which instinctively worked for me, an incredible shot in the arm at a time when concerts elsewhere in London seemed to be getting more difficult. Quite why I had struck gold when others had failed was never absolutely clear to me. I was described later as the man who pre-packaged concerts, doing for music what Marks and Spencer did for food – I was never quite sure whether that was intended as a compliment. I took risks and developed new ideas. Whatever it was, it certainly put me well and truly on the map.

Within eighteen months of the Barbican's opening, I was promoting about 125 concerts and events a year. This included some lunchtime concerts, which proved very popular at the time and one actually sold out, which was amazing for a venue seating more than two thousand. Turning people away at lunchtime was an entirely new sensation which I rather enjoyed.

One evening, about a year after the complex opened, I attended an event at the Barbican hosted by the City of London, to celebrate something or other. 'I often come here to concerts,' said a rather stuffy lady. 'Not to yours, of course,' she added, addressing me. 'You are lowering the tone, young man, that's what you are doing.'

Such a sentiment was not entirely unknown but seldom expressed quite so clearly or directly. I was doing what you are not supposed to do, making money from concerts of classical music. Yet the view persisted in some quarters that the only people who were entitled to earn real money were the artists; the enterprise overall was expected to lose money. That is why there was an Arts Council with its endless committees doling out public funds to support the arts. Yet there was I, in the newly opened Barbican, snapping up as many dates as I could, and filling the place three of four times a week with symphony concerts, opera galas, Tchaikovsky evenings and the rest.

So I'm afraid I didn't care two hoots what people said, I was doing what I had always been doing, enjoying myself. To actually be able to earn my living from doing something I loved was an added bonus. The real icing on the cake was cocking a snook at the Establishment and selling all the seats.

The Barbican now accounted for nearly three quarters of my business. The symphony concerts alone, about fifty a year, provided an alternative popular series to the more heavyweight offerings of the LSO. Their managing director, Peter Hemmings, had joined them after a stormy period with Opera Australia. Previously, I had remembered him as an extremely patronising head of Scottish Opera. Now he invited me to lunch at the Garrick Club, a place where the same coterie of actors and hangers-on always seem to remain by the bar until relieved, eventually, by an obituary in *The Times*.

Anyway, here I was back with school lunch at the Garrick and the headmaster, Peter Hemmings, more or less demanding that I restrict my activities at the Barbican to no more than ten concerts a year. I looked at him in amazement; he was already doing a fantastic job at bringing the orchestra close to bankruptcy with poor planning and bad programming and was now trying to push the blame for his own inadequacies onto me. How could he possibly expect to find an audience for five performances in a single week of Berlioz's *Harold in Italy*, to give just one obvious example of his crazy planning? Later, the LSO went to the other extreme and I found many of my potential programmes clashing with theirs as we all raced to register with the hall our respective choice of the popular concertos and symphonies.

Not surprisingly, Henry Wrong and his team had no interest in subscribing to Hemmings' request and it was not long before Hemmings himself left the LSO. He moved on to run the opera in Los Angeles and returned to the UK on his retirement and was appointed to the board of the Royal Opera House in 2000 in time for the post-development reopening. I learnt later that he had vetoed my being invited to the reopening for which I would have been expected to pay a large sum for the tickets. I wore the veto as yet another badge of honour.

It was around this time that I was having one of my fairly regular catch-up lunches with Henry when he asked me what I thought had gone wrong with the LSO. So I started enumerating various points, finishing up by saying that I thought they were very arrogant. I had noticed when I started reciting my list that Henry took out a piece of paper and began scribbling away. That afternoon, I subsequently learnt, Henry went to a meeting with the LSO. He said there were a number of issues he wished to raise with them and, pulling a piece of paper from his pocket, proceeded to lambast them by quoting the points I had made over our lunch, finishing up by saying, 'And, finally, you are very arrogant.'

Then, as so often happens, a saviour emerged, in this case a cellist in the LSO who also ran an antiques shop in Hampstead. I had known him first from my Sunday evening concerts at the Pier Theatre, Bournemouth, many years previously, when, on occasion, he replaced the regular cellist in the trio accompanying the singers. He had the daunting task of getting the LSO back on its feet, which he achieved with great success. It is no wonder that he has ended up with a knighthood as Sir Clive Gillinson, the head of Carnegie Hall in New York.

Working as the head of a self-governing orchestra of up to one hundred musicians is no simple task. I suspect there was a great deal of respect for him from the players at the LSO once he started to get results but assuaging the egos and concerns of that number of players who had known him previously as one of their body cannot have been easy. The players were unnerved by the poor level of business at their new home and the Barbican itself did not make things any easier when it emerged that Henry Wrong had had at least one clandestine meeting with the manager of another of the London orchestras on the subject of whether they might like to replace the LSO at the Barbican. The LSO has much to thank Clive for; he clearly had a very good business brain and a capacity to rebuild confidence in the orchestra itself and in its audiences.

The early days at the Barbican were truly remarkable. The buzz and the excitement are hard to describe now, with the advance box office receipts moving strongly upwards every day. One day, I was standing in the box office before one of my concerts and picked up a ringing telephone as everyone else was deeply immersed in selling tickets, many of them mine. 'Hello,' a voice said. 'I've reached Margate — how do I get to you?'

'Surely you mean Moorgate?' I enquired. But alas, no, they had headed off to the Isle of Thanet thinking this was where the Barbican was situated.

There were many strange and amusing incidents during those early days at the centre. On one occasion, at an all-Beethoven programme with the RPO, a steward found a couple, between the double doors leading into the auditorium, *in flagrante*. When I later mentioned this to the duty house manager, he turned to me and said, without the flicker of a smile, 'They must have been latecomers.' A few days later, I overheard somebody ask at the box office, 'What have you got on tonight?' Which drew the not too helpful response, 'Grey trousers, a white shirt and a blue jacket.'

Box office humour is a law unto itself, as unique as the characters who run the box offices. Over at the South Bank, the box office manager at the Royal Festival Hall for many years was Bob Howden, a former naval master-at-arms. His proud boast was that he had never actually been to see anything at the hall itself. On days when the box office was busy, the telephone was left unanswered save for a recorded message which asked callers to ring again on another day. One day, Bob forgot to turn on the message and the phone kept ringing and ringing, so he picked it up and said, 'This is a recorded announcement from the box office at the Royal Festival Hall. As we are unable owing to pressure of business to attend to telephone bookings today, please call again tomorrow.' A voice at the other end started to question the details, so Bob replied, 'I've already told you, this is a recorded announcement from the box office at the Royal Festival Hall.' Sadly there is no record of exactly how the conversation was brought to a close.

In response to numerous complaints that it was difficult to find the centre on foot, the Barbican quite early on painted yellow lines showing the route to follow from the outlying parts of the complex to the Barbican Centre itself. In the first year of opening, there was a cold winter, with some snow and ice. Two old ladies were attending one of my concerts and were following the yellow line into the centre. It was a fairly bright, moonlit evening and the lines were reflected by the ice which had formed in the lake by the side of the Barbican. The two old dears walked onto the ice and fell into the water but the Barbican's proud boast was that they were fished out and dried in time for the start of the concert. The RSC even lent a hand by drying out their clothes in the theatre wardrobe.

In the summer of 1983, the Barbican suddenly found itself with virtually no concerts in August. The previous year, the LSO had presented a series of open-air concerts on the Sculpture Court with the fall-back position of being able to move them into the Concert Hall in the event of bad weather but they had decided for whatever reason that they were not going to do this any more. The planning manager asked me if I would take on some dates in what was traditionally a very quiet month. He said that the Barbican would be happy to take just a small share of the box office instead of the normal rental and he mentioned a figure of ten per cent. I thought he had gone totally mad as this was almost tantamount to giving the venue away. Fortunately, I was always programmed to respond with a counter offer – it never makes sense to say yes straight away. So I found myself saying, whilst managing not to grin, 'What about five per cent?' I ended up agreeing to take four dates at five per cent.

As I left, I bumped into Henry Wrong who said, 'Raymond, what a shame the LSO is not doing anything in August. If you take some dates, we will give you the hall for nothing.' I called the planning manager back when I reached the office and told him of my conversation with Henry. He was shocked and said that Henry had no authority to offer free dates. Nevertheless, I ended up with a total of six dates for which the Barbican took just three per cent of the box office receipts. All six sold out.

My business there was going from strength to strength. Alongside the symphonic concerts and the opera galas, the Barbican gave me the opportunity to try out lots of new ideas. Here at last was a venue in central London with enough seats to make many projects viable, with car parking alongside and decent bars and restaurants. Of course, not everyone was happy; the critics carped at its location but the public flocked to it.

I started working there regularly with Victor Borge and I did several concerts with Henry Mancini. I even co-presented a complete Beethoven Cycle with the RPO under Sir Charles Groves and repeated it a couple of years later. These were exciting times with constant press speculation as to what would happen with the LSO. Eventually, better planning and bigger grants enabled them to stabilise their position at the Barbican. I knew they were back on top when they no longer wanted to take engagements from me as they did not feel that they needed to be seen to be doing my dates, thereby perhaps diluting their rising profile at the Barbican.

In 1984, I had a call from a concert agent with whom I dealt saying that Edward Heath had indicated he wanted to conduct some concerts with a young cellist. So a meeting was arranged at Mr Heath's London residence and this time I went there in my own right and not as somebody's chauffeur. A very private individual, Heath had no discernible personal or social life; a conversation with him was always rather stilted and inevitably led up to him talking about himself. He made it appear all the way through that he was not sure that he really wanted to do the concerts and that I would have to persuade him. His attitude throughout was geared as though he expected me to plead with him but Jewish lads from north-west London don't do that kind of thing! The meeting ended inconclusively with Mr Heath indicating that he would have to think about it.

A few days later, I had a call from the agent. Where, she wanted to know, was the offer for Mr Heath? He was keen as mustard and was simply waiting for my formal offer. So I put together half a dozen dates including one at the Barbican. As a courtesy, I dropped a note to Henry Wrong. A couple of days later I had an anguished call from him telling me that he had replied to my letter but he wanted me to destroy his letter unopened. The next morning, I rushed early to the office and grabbed the post before anybody else had had a chance to look at it. I easily located Henry's letter in the Barbican envelope with its distinctive logo and I destroyed it, but not before I had a peep at it. It said something to the effect that he hoped Mr Heath would make a better conductor than he had a prime minister although he doubted it. In the event, his hopes were realised — Mr Heath was a marginally better conductor.

At the first rehearsal, I was surprised to see Mr Heath changing his shirt six times, something I had never witnessed before. Unlike Prince Andrew, who much more recently famously claimed in his interview on the Jeffrey Epstein affair that he never sweated at all, Heath was quite the opposite. We rehearsed the overture and he was off changing, the same thing happened after the concerto and so on. Was it thus that the nation's business was decided?

I got chatting to his detective during rehearsals. The poor man was permanently attached to Heath and had to go everywhere with him. He clearly was not too fond of music although he said that our programme was rather more acceptable than his visit the previous year 'to Beirut', or at least that is how he pronounced it. Apparently, the visit to Bayreuth for the *Ring Cycle* was so successful that Mr Heath decided to stay on for performances of *Parsifal* and 'that Dutchman thing', as the detective put it. I found it wise thereafter not to mention Wagner to the detective.

All the dates on the tour were within easy reach of London. Business was not particularly good except in Chichester where the audience at the Festival Theatre was largely of an age that might have confused reality and imagination. I swear many of them thought that Mr Heath was still prime minister. At the Barbican, I was struck by the fact that nobody came round to see him afterwards apart from his housekeeper. I took him to a local Italian restaurant for a post-concert supper. He was not an easy man to converse with but fortunately he was again kept busy talking about his one favourite subject, himself.

The last date on the tour was at Dartford and Mr Heath invited me for a meal in between the rehearsal and the concert. It was memorable mainly for the incredibly fast driving by his chauffeur who either had, or thought he had, special dispensation to weave in and out of the traffic on the dual carriageway that took us into Mr Heath's adjoining constituency. I never quite fully understood why Mr Heath had wanted to conduct the handsome young cellist in the series of concerts and nobody ever explained.

About the same time as the tour, I was asked if I might be interested in presenting Ivo Pogorelich at the Barbican. He had enjoyed a meteoric rise and was now living in London with his Georgian-born wife who looked old enough to be his grandmother. *The Sunday Times* carried an article with photographs of them and the interest at the box office was enormous. Pogorelich's style was idiosyncratic, not beloved by all the critics but he had a very large public following. He was tall with longish blond hair and youthful if calculated charm. At the Barbican, he pounded the piano in such a way that he managed to break a string which had to be repaired and added to the drama.

Some weeks later, I was invited for lunch at the Pogorelichs' apartment in Mayfair. His wife had taken to calling me 'Gubbay, Gubbay' — perhaps this was a Georgian way of greeting, I am not sure, but I found it quite endearing. 'Gubbay, Gubbay, come to lunch,' she had said, and so there I was sampling her celebrated Georgian chicken. I could not help but notice that the kitchen was bespattered with the stains of chicken fat and grease, clearly the result of preparing this dish so often.

Pogorelich succeeded in appearing at just one out of the three subsequent concerts arranged for him at the Barbican, citing illness in each case. By this point, both I and the insurers felt that we had had enough. I bumped into him some years later at the Royal Festival Hall during a recital by Montserrat Caballe. A familiar voice called across the foyer, 'Gubbay, Gubbay.'

Ivo managed to be both charming and cutting at the same time as he said, 'Poor Montserrat, she is so ill. You can tell it, can't you?'

'Yes,' said Mrs Pogorelich. 'Gubbay, Gubbay, you can tell it.'

I heard some time later that Mrs Pogorelich had died, which was sad news; I really did warm to her.

One of the other big moments in the early days of the Barbican came from the opportunity to present *Napoleon*. This truly epic silent film directed by Abel Gance in 1929 had been researched and reconstructed by film historian Kevin Brownlow. It had been shown in the 1982 London Film Festival at the Empire, Leicester Square, with live orchestral accompaniment in a score partly arranged and written by Carl Davis. Now there was a chance to stage it at the Barbican for two performances. The film in its present form ran for well over six hours and so the first performance was given in two parts on a Thursday and Friday evening with the second performance on the Saturday afternoon and evening with a lengthy interval in between. I say 'present form' because originally it had been even longer.

Gance had intended this as the first part of a six-part series on the life of Napoleon but he spent so long on the first part that the money ran out and he was not able to continue with the project. The film was eventually shown in a greatly edited version and much of the original material was either lost or misplaced but Brownlow's research over several years had resulted in a much fuller version, including the astonishing triptych in the closing minutes when the screen suddenly opens out to reveal three separate images running side by side. This and so many other techniques pioneered by Gance were revolutionary and had a lasting effect on the development of cinema.

Even after he had prepared the reconstructed version, Kevin Brownlow was still adding in newly discovered material. Carl Davis's score relied heavily on using existing, largely symphonic, music of the period so there was lots of Mozart, Haydn and the composers associated with the French Revolution such as Mehul and Gretry. Above all, there was Beethoven, with huge chunks taken from his symphonies and other works. Clearly not everyone shared my enthusiasm for either the film or the music. A review of an orchestral concert in 1986 by Richard Morrison in *The Times* started:

The last time I saw Carl Davis in charge of an orchestra he had cut up some rather revered music by Beethoven into small bits, pasted them together in a different order, added a liberal sprinkling of repeat marks, and was using this papier mâché masterpiece to accompany an interminable silent movie called Napoleon. Now he has been appointed associate conductor of the London Philharmonic Orchestra. One trusts that his new responsibilities will not include wielding the scissors too often on Beethoven. So our only problem is what he does with his baton. This was the blandest music-making I have heard since I inadvertently caught the James Last Orchestra on television.

Carl Davis's great ability was to match the mood of the drama with appropriate music and to sustain the sense of musical unity over the entire length of the film. He had also written original music, including the 'Eagle' theme for Napoleon himself. The whole score was impressive but the musical side led to enormous difficulties with regard to the cost of mounting performances of the film. Although commissioned by Thames Television, the entire rights in the score had been vested in Carl Davis and his publisher had cannily registered the piece in such a way that it was covered by a Grand Rights agreement. This meant that it was impossible to perform the piece under the normal Performing Rights License held by each venue. This greatly increased the cost of putting on performances. It also meant that the seat prices had to be very high for what was perceived by the audience as just a silent film with musical accompaniment. That is not in any way to underplay Carl Davis's contribution to the success of the film but it was very difficult for audiences to comprehend the economics of mounting the special showings.

At this time, I also worked quite often with Nigel Kennedy, in the days when he had a Christian name as well as a surname and he was happy to turn up for a *Four Seasons* or whatever. The last time I booked him, his agent called me a couple of days before the concert to say that Nigel had decided he was not well enough to do the engagement. I could not really get to the bottom of what was actually wrong with him. Eventually, I sent a fax saying that I would have to ask Nigel to attend, at my expense, a specialist in Harley Street for a medical examination. The mystery malady disappeared as quickly as it had arisen and Nigel did the concert. I could not quite bring myself to ask him how he was but he played beautifully.

At the very first concert with the newly formed London Concert Orchestra at the Queen Elizabeth Hall back in 1972, the first clarinet player was Jack Brymer. Jack was a self-taught player who started life as a schoolmaster before Beecham summoned him to join the RPO in its fledgling days. For more than fifty years he delighted and charmed audiences and colleagues with both his virtuoso playing and his genial stories about conductors and musicians. Quite why he had accepted the booking I will never know. He was the leading player of his generation and had just left the BBC Symphony Orchestra and was about to join the LSO.

I went on to work with him often at the Barbican; his silvery playing of the Mozart Clarinet Concerto in particular was thrilling. A pure, rich, beautifully phrased account, which always pleased the large audiences that came to see him. He was still with the LSO and, at the time of one of his solo engagements for me, the BBC was halfway through transmitting a four-part series it had recorded about the orchestra. Jack was finished playing by the interval and wanted to go home but Joan, his wife, suggested they stay and watch that evening's programme which was about to be shown. There was a television set in the backstage area conveniently placed by the artists' bar. Jack was not keen but Joan insisted and so we all sat down to watch.

Shortly after the start, Jack was shown leaving his house for rehearsals. 'Oh, Jack,' said Joan, 'you're wearing your smart overcoat. Did you put that on for the camera?' Jack shuffled awkwardly and muttered, 'No, of course not.' Then a little later, Jack was shown gardening at home. 'Oh, Jack, you don't normally put that nice jacket on when you prune the roses. Did you do it for the camera?' More awkward shuffling and protestations followed.

Jack continued to work right up to his eightieth birthday and I was thrilled to be able to put on a birthday concert for him at the Barbican. He played the Mozart, of course, and the Weber and more besides. It was a happy occasion with many of his friends and colleagues turning up. I had arranged for the actor Timothy West, a fan of Jack's and a great music-lover, to appear as a surprise guest at the end and to present Jack with a special cake, baked by Jane Asher, in the shape of, well, it had to be, a clarinet.

Conductors also played a major part in the early years at the Barbican. With up to 130 concerts a year, we needed quite a supply of them. Marcus Dods conducted most of the London Concert Orchestra dates and, at one point, he had conducted many more concerts at the Barbican than any other conductor. But then, two years after the centre opened, he died of cancer. A wartime bomber pilot of distinction, a marvellous, versatile musician, he had been enormously helpful and encouraging to me at a time when I was moving from smaller-scale events to full orchestral concerts. At his memorial concert at the Barbican, Josephine Barstow sang Faure's *Requiem* and Sir David Willcocks, an old wartime colleague, conducted.

Norman del Mar also conducted several of our early concerts there, though I always felt he thought it all a little beneath him to have to conduct for my type of concert. One of the last he did for me was with the violinist, Oscar Shumsky, who had become something of a cult figure amongst fellow violinists. He was a renowned player with a virtuoso technique but public appearances by him especially in London were quite rare. After playing a Mozart concerto in the first half, he opened the second with Saint-Saens's *Introduction and Rondo Capriccioso.* Norman conducted with his usual vigour and, on the reprise of the big melody, literally jumped up in the air off the podium. Shumsky played an encore after which half the audience, or so it seemed, departed, several of them carrying violin cases. Such was Shumsky's fame that so many of the capital's leading players were keen to see him live. It was a much depleted audience that stayed to hear Norman carve his way through Beethoven's *Symphony No. 8.*

Maurice Handford, who had had a long association with the Halle Orchestra in Manchester, also conducted several of the early symphony concerts, including one memorable occasion with John Ogdon. John had won first prize in the Tchaikovsky Competition in Moscow in 1962, which set him on the path of a glittering career. However, he had been *hors de combat* following a breakdown in 1973 and had spent much time in the Maudsley Hospital in London. From 1983 onwards, he was allowed out to play the odd concert. Maurice came off after the concerto looking completely shaken. John Ogdon, always an idiosyncratic player, had pulled the concerto to pieces and raced towards the final bars. Poor Maurice had had a terrible job trying to keep up with him.

John Ogdon appeared many times for me, initially arriving with his 'minders' from the institution where he was living. Later he was allowed out on his own but he was never permitted to have any money as he was still an undischarged bankrupt. All his fees went directly to the receiver in bankruptcy. I once found him wandering around backstage long after the interval when he would normally have left. He was waiting, he told me, for the rain to end so that he could go to the bus stop without getting soaked. It seemed a cruel turn of fate that someone so talented, having thrilled a capacity audience at the Barbican, many with expensive cars parked in the adjoining car parks, had to wait in the rain for a bus to take him home. I was delighted to order a pre-paid taxi for him. I was extremely sad to hear in 1989 that he had died. A great bear of a man with an enormous talent and a winning smile, he deserved rather better out of life. I treasure the fact that I worked with him.

Another conductor who came my way was Martin Fischer-Dieskau, son of the great baritone, Dietrich. He was a tall, personable, young man and not a bad conductor. Rather like John Heddle Nash, he had chosen to keep his distinctive surname that immediately made sure he was noticed but also brought with it the not-always-helpful attention of the critics. At the last concert he did for me at the Barbican, he suddenly complained just before the start that he was not well and he retired to the dressing room where he stretched his six-foot-or-more frame out on the couch. Barry Griffiths, at that time the RPO's leader, was marvellous. He arrived in the dressing room at 7.29pm, violin and bow in hand, and said, 'Maestro, everything is fine. I will go on and start the concert and you can join us when you are ready.' Whatever the ailment, it was suddenly cured as Fischer-Diskau leapt to his feet and announced there would be no need for Barry to start as he was after all feeling much improved and would now be able to undertake the concert.

Richard Hickox, James Judd and Yan Pascal Tortelier all conducted on a reasonably regular basis for me at the Barbican during its first two or three years and the soloists included Cecile Ousset, Stephen Hough, Cristina Ortiz and Peter Donohoe. In fact, it was Peter who was the soloist on the occasion when the piano lift got stuck. The lift delivers the piano right onto the concert platform and has delighted audiences with the sudden delivery of the Steinway in the middle of the stage ever since the centre opened. It was a particular novelty early on when not many people were aware of it and the sight of the piano suddenly rising up invariably drew a round of applause.

This time, the piano failed to appear; well, that is not quite true, its top appeared and those seated higher up would have been able to catch sight of a little more of it, but there it stood, stuck fast. The lift mechanism had broken down. A speedy change of programme meant that we rescheduled the symphony that was to close the concert to a position before the interval. Then, during the interval, the Barbican's backstage team, aided by volunteers from the RPO and even some sturdy members of the audience, manhandled the instrument out of the open lift shaft and onto the stage. Steinway's tuner was able to check the instrument in record time and a very game Peter

Donohoe gave a cracking performance of Beethoven's *Emperor Concerto* on a stage with a giant rectangular hole left in it. Around it, members of the RPO string section tried desperately not to fall in.

Although I worked with all four London orchestras, my closest association was with the Royal Philharmonic to which Ian Maclay had returned as chief executive shortly before the Barbican opening. Ian is one of the great characters in the orchestral world, a manager with a sense of humour and fun, a practical frame of mind and a decided lack of the usual bulls**t that normally accompanies such characters. He was very much from the glass-half-full school of thought and would never tire of finding ways to make things work. I had known him in a much more junior capacity in the 1970s when he was often fielded to deflect enquiries over unpaid artists' fees at a time when the small concert agency, which I also ran at that time, represented several soloists engaged by the RPO. In the meantime, Ian had been working at the South Bank as planning manager. Now he was in charge of the RPO and determined to keep it busy with a full diary. We spoke virtually every day and very often some Barbican dates would come in at relatively short notice which required immediate programming and booking of artists. We would always be doing deals together, Ian trying to get me to engage conductors and soloists to whom he owed favours in return for quoting me attractive rates for the orchestra.

Many artists and conductors found financial backing for making recordings but demanded live concerts in return. Thus Ian would need to find them engagements and concerts at the Barbican were extremely useful to him. Ian had the kind of dogged enthusiasm which would almost always lead to us closing the deal. There is one particular example that we both still vividly remember. The Barbican suddenly offered me three dates in September 1982, just six months after the opening. Two of these were weekdays, much less attractive than the key weekend dates. Ian was persuasive and eventually we agreed one single fee for the three dates, one of which could have a 'Bolero-sized' orchestra.

Symphony orchestras come in different shapes and sizes depending on the repertoire. So for Ravel's *Bolero*, the orchestra is huge — full wind and brass plus saxophones and a lot of percussion. At the other end, there is the

Mozart-sized orchestra and, somewhere in the middle, the more conventional-sized band. So the cost of hiring a symphony orchestra can vary enormously and what Ian was prepared to do here was to quote an attractive global figure covering all three concerts with the varying number of players. This was very much a bonus as it enabled me to programme Ravel's *Bolero*, normally an expensive option on account of the extra players needed to perform this piece. All three concerts did extremely well including one, with Julian Lloyd Webber playing Elgar's *Cello Concerto*, which required no advertising at all – it sold entirely from the entry in the Barbican's monthly diary of events. That was a rare occasion even then; sadly, now it would be impossible.

On another occasion, the soloists included a young singer, Anna Steiger. The backstage supervisor was surprised to receive a call during 'the half' – the thirty-five minute period before the start time – asking to be put through to her. When he asked who was calling, he was told it was her father and then the penny dropped, it was Rod Steiger on the line, Anna's dad. On another occasion, when we were staging concert performances of *Jesus Christ Superstar*, Freddie Mercury arrived backstage with his minder to see one of the cast.

Those early days at the Barbican were extraordinary. It was like defying gravity. Here was I doing literally hundreds of concerts, bringing in huge audiences and making money out of it. The Arts Council, I subsequently found out, tried every angle to explain why this phenomenon was unique to the Barbican and could not be used as a model for anywhere else. In a sense they were right, commercial concerts do only work in certain circumstances and with certain types of repertoire. I could move swiftly, without the weight of accountability to anyone but myself, and follow my nose. I was programming what some saw as 'musical lollipops' – or, in other words, music that people wanted to come to the Barbican to hear. There is an art to balancing programmes and getting the right combination but it also requires simple common sense. I was not surprised, for example, when Berlioz's *Harold in Italy* given five times in a week by the LSO failed to draw the crowds. But it left the way clear for the likes of me and I had a wonderful time rattling the Establishment's cage.

Around this time, a critical situation in former Yugoslavia, where the country had split up into its former state of several smaller countries, led to the sudden announcement of a charity concert organised by a group of artists' agents at very short notice, which the Prince and Princess of Wales would attend. Peter Skinner in the box office had to arrange tickets to be on sale in record time. The concert was sold out and raised a substantial sum for the charity. The following morning, I could not resist calling Peter, mimicking Henry Wrong's voice, which I had learnt to copy.

'Peter,' I said, 'it's Henry. Everybody was so thrilled with last night that we are going to repeat it again in a week's time.'

Peter was completely confused, 'But Mr Wrong,' he said, 'I'm not sure we can get it all together in time.' I confessed it was me making the call and Peter was more relieved than angry, which was just as well as he was a rock on which I relied.

It was also during the early years of the Barbican that I started to develop the Christmas Festival. The centre had found nobody to take the post-Christmas dates between Boxing Day and New Year's Eve, when the LSO had its Viennese programme. So I linked these to the pre-Christmas dates I already had and started to plan a series of afternoon and evening performances with a variety of different, largely seasonal programmes. I had an approach from Howard Blake, who had just recorded a new children's piece he had written. Bernard Cribbens had narrated Raymond Brigg's story of *The Snowman* which Howard had set to music. So I scheduled an afternoon performance and coupled it with *Peter and the Wolf* as it was otherwise only one half of the programme. It went very well and I decided to repeat it the following year. In the late summer, I had a call from Howard. Did I know, he asked, that Aled Jones had recorded the song from *The Snowman*, 'Walking in the Air'? Could we book him for Christmas?

Aled Jones had appeared quite suddenly on the music scene. A boy soprano from North Wales of quite outstanding ability, he had, I discovered, already been snapped up by one of the London concert agents who was demanding a high fee but, yes, I could book him. Even before we got to our Christmas Festival, I had added an extra performance of *The Snowman*. Aled's voice was extraordinary; I had heard a lot of boy sopranos but never anything quite like this. It was extremely powerful and had a depth and timbre which made it very special. The following Christmas, Aled's voice had still not broken and I arranged another series, perhaps four performances, of *The Snowman* at the Barbican.

The piece continued for some years as a regular part of the Barbican Christmas Festival but alas, of course, Aled was no longer able to take part. A few years later, he did return, only this time as narrator, a fine young man but still unmistakably Aled. His soft Welsh voice spoke the lines but this time the boy soprano was English – young Anthony Mellor, the son of the former cabinet minister David Mellor. He had a perfectly acceptable boy soprano voice of what I would describe as the English church tradition. Nothing, however, could efface the memories of young Aled.

About the same time, I had put together the Teddy Bear Concerts, where children were admitted at a lower price if they brought their teddy bears with them. These proved wildly successful and I ran them at Christmastime for several years. For the first few years, Michael Bond appeared as a surprise guest with Paddington Bear.

For quite a long while it seemed that the Barbican was on a roll but dark clouds were beginning to form on the horizon.

CHAPTER TEN

THE BARONESS AND
THE BARBICAN

Henry Wrong had done a great job in getting the Barbican open and steering it through very difficult times to establish it as one of the world's major arts centres. He took total credit for everything but he had an incredible team behind him, headed by his deputy, Richard York, who had given him huge support and without whom the centre might never have opened. Richard had come to the Barbican from the Royal Shakespeare Company about six years before the opening. Although steeped in theatre when he arrived, he also very quickly got to grips with the vagaries of the musical world and spent a lot of time sorting out and smoothing over the wrinkles that inevitably flowed from Henry's broad-brushstroke approach.

However, in 1988, after six years of Henry's stewardship following the opening, as well as a dozen prior to this, the City Fathers on the Corporation decided they wanted a change and Henry was pensioned off on full salary. Henry was not in the end uncomfortable with the deal he had struck with the City Corporation and I think they were happy too that the contract provided for confidentiality, which was not one of Henry's natural traits.

Henry had made it no secret that he felt he should be awarded a knighthood and maybe he did deserve one, given the long period of unsure gestation before the centre eventually opened and his work afterwards to make it such a success. When he was eventually awarded a CBE, I telephoned him to offer him my congratulations, adding, with an almost imperceptible twinkle, 'But it's not enough.'

'Raymond,' he said, 'you are so right.'

The choice of his successor was of particular interest to me as I was still doing the greater part of my promoting work at the Barbican. The eventual shortlist included Henry's deputy, Richard York, and Detta O'Cathain, formerly of the Milk Marketing Board. Richard was an obvious successor and a very reliable, safe pair of hands, much respected by the Barbican team and its many clients. Maybe that is why he was passed over for somebody with no previous experience of arts administration.

The Milk Marketing Board was a million miles away from the Barbican but somehow the Corporation of the City of London believed that the centre could be run more commercially and needed the hand of an outsider at the helm to hold back the excesses, as it perceived them, of the arts establishment. This was a very clear signal from the City that things were changing at the Barbican. Putting in an outsider with no obvious practical knowledge of how an arts centre functioned appeared to be very deliberate and, as it turned out, high risk. It was rather like chucking out the baby with the bathwater.

Henry and the team who worked with him had already moved things on substantially from the original scenario, under which the City believed that the centre could be virtually self-sufficient with income from conferences and exhibitions cross-funding some of the activities in the concert hall. Unfortunately, this ambition was somewhat hamstrung by the fact that the conference business potential was never that great and the exhibition halls were converted car parks with poor facilities. The cumulative effect left a big hole in the budget.

The Royal Shakespeare Company was at this time in residence at the theatre and was supported financially by both the City and the Arts Council. In the concert hall, the London Symphony Orchestra also enjoyed funding from both of these bodies. To its credit, the City started to fund programming beyond the RSC and the LSO and, eventually, the Arts Council too began to support the Barbican Centre directly as well as continuing to support the resident organisations.

As a commercial promoter, I was always on the outside when it came to funding. I did not need it, which annoyed some of my subsidy-supported colleagues who could not understand how it was possible to make money out of classical music. Victor Hochhauser, my old 'friend', true to form, claimed that I was losing money on every event I promoted. He had clung on to his Sunday nights at the Royal Albert Hall until he was forced to take notice of the Barbican and started asking for dates there. The competition did not worry me, even though at times he seemed to slavishly borrow many of my programme ideas. I just had to keep one step ahead all the time.

At my first meeting with Detta, it was clear to me that she knew little about either how the arts functioned generally or specifically about running an arts centre. She was, however, determined to instil stern financial control into what she saw as a loosely run, artistically led enterprise that needed to be brought to heel. This was not a fair assessment of the Barbican before her arrival but nonetheless one she seemed determined to portray. This was presumably the same line taken by her political masters, for it was clear that she had their undivided support. Richard York, who had worked so long and hard taking care of so much during Henry's period of control, suddenly found himself sidelined. Then began the sackings.

Loyal and hard-working members of the team suddenly found themselves out of work. All the *esprit de corps* that had been a hallmark of the Barbican from its earliest days simply vanished. Enthusiasm was replaced by fear. Thursday afternoon was the time for the chop and if you survived through to Friday, you knew you were safe for at least another week. Richard York was eventually dismissed and I wrote to Detta suggesting that his long and loyal service should at least be recognised in some way. When she next saw me backstage, she rounded on me, accusing me of interfering in the internal affairs of the centre. I pointed out I had merely made a suggestion which seemed highly appropriate. After all, Richard had been at the Barbican for fifteen years and his contribution to its success certainly deserved proper recognition and acknowledgement. Peter Skinner, our box office stalwart, who, with his sister Eileen, had moved over from the Aldwych to run the box office for the whole of the Barbican Centre was another victim. He had enthusiastically embraced the world of computer box office systems with much success but was unceremoniously dismissed. Other loyal, hard-working members of the original team vanished almost overnight.

The mood of the centre changed dramatically. In a place of entertainment where the atmosphere should be welcoming and inviting, frightened faces and sunken eyes greeted the public. Then, quite suddenly, Detta was made a baroness and, perhaps somewhat insensitively, included the Barbican in her title. To my surprise, Detta's initial contract was extended by the City, who appeared totally oblivious as to what was actually going on at the Barbican.

After she had been reappointed, I found myself talking round the problems one day over lunch with my old cellist friend Clive Gillinson, now the managing director of the London Symphony Orchestra. It was very clear by what neither of us actually said that we both had rather similar views. In a move that still makes me very proud, a few days later I effectively lit the blue touch-paper. I went to see Richard Morrison at *The Times*, then out at Wapping. In an article celebrating the LSO's ninetieth birthday, which appeared in the newspaper a few days later, Richard tagged a couple of sentences on at the end, mentioning the problems at the Barbican. This was the first public observation about the serious situation that had been swelling up at the centre.

Some days later, this was followed by another, more focused piece, again by Richard Morrison. Other papers started to dig and, eventually, a tidal wave exploded in the press, which forced the City to act. At first, the Corporation refused to accept that anything was seriously amiss and tried to smooth over the situation by talking to the resident organisations at the Barbican. Apparently, neither the London Symphony Orchestra nor the Royal Shakespeare Company was in any mood to be mollified. The culmination of all this was a tsunami of critical articles in the national press, followed swiftly by the Baroness's departure, which was summed up with the headline in the *Evening Standard* in November 1994: 'Amazing Scenes at the Barbican as Baroness Is Told: Go Now', and in the *Telegraph*: 'Baroness Ousted from the Barbican'.

By the time I received a call from the Corporation's Barbican committee chairman, the mood had changed. I was merely asked to give a frank appraisal of what I thought had been going wrong. I did not particularly like having to talk quite so openly but there was little choice. There was no getting away from the fact that staff morale had sunk to an all-time low. It really was the case of a square peg in a round hole. She never seemed very comfortable in the job and words had to be chosen with care. The Baroness departed and the Barbican came back to life. The nine silly statues of the

Muses cast in fibreglass, which had been placed on the Silk Street canopy as part of the 1994 centre refurbishment, and which seemed to signify her era, found themselves sold off at a substantial loss to the City. I am told that they now reside in South Africa, perched outside a winery.

One of the few events of mine which the Baroness attended was the first of a pair of concerts with Victor Borge. He liked the centre and I had already presented him there on several occasions. He used to do a gag where he walked with his hand-held microphone towards the opposite side of the stage and it snagged. This deliberate little trick allowed him to turn to the audience and exclaim that although the centre had cost so many millions of pounds, for a few pennies more they could have afforded to buy a proper lead for the microphone. The audience used to laugh at another example of his carefully contrived, deadpan humour. Not, however, the Baroness. She came round at the end of the performance to be introduced and told Borge that she was terribly embarrassed by what had happened with the microphone and she would make quite sure that it was put right for the following evening. Borge, who had a ready quip for every situation, was for once absolutely speechless, the only time I ever witnessed him lost for words.

When Detta O'Cathain departed, the City Chamberlain, Bernard Harty, took over on a temporary basis whilst a replacement was found. Eventually, John Tusa, formerly Controller of the BBC World Service, took over with Graham Sheffield, another former BBC employee but by then working at the South Bank Centre, as his deputy, restoring morale and a sense of purpose to the beleaguered organisation.

The more recent history of the Barbican has been much more settled and stable under their leadership and subsequently that of Nicholas Kenyon. The programming has changed enormously in the nearly forty years since it opened but it is still an exciting and interesting venue. The Barbican will always have an important place in my affection. In spite of all the carping over the years about its position and its awkwardly sited main entrance, it remains a special place for me. It was the City's gift to the nation, and London and the whole country are by far the better for having it. In spite of the criticisms, it has provided London and its visitors with a complete arts centre and brought cultural life right to the heart of the City. With an art gallery, library, cinemas and a small theatre as well as the main theatre and the concert hall, it has become part of the very fabric of the cultural heritage of the nation's capital city.

The City and the London Symphony Orchestra have now abandoned plans to build a new hall on the site of the present Museum of London. If they had done so, it would no doubt have been an exciting and interesting development but it could never measure up to those heady days in the early 1980s after the Barbican first opened its doors. If they must provide a new home for the LSO, all they really need to do is to tow Symphony Hall – the most wonderful concert hall we have in this country – from Birmingham the 110 miles to the City of London. Now that really would be a magnificent prospect.

Returning for a moment to Victor Borge, I had booked him for an appearance with the Royal Philharmonic at the Barbican as he enjoyed on occasion working with an orchestra, rather than just doing his usual solo performance. The night before, he had appeared on television being interviewed by Sue Lawley. Another guest was Vladimir Ashkenazy, at that time musical director of the RPO. Ashkenazy picked up that Borge was appearing the following night at the Barbican but not that the RPO was playing for him. In fact, he had asked the RPO management specifically to avoid taking on any engagements in between his rehearsals and performances. A request to which they clearly paid scant notice.

The next day, Ashkenazy arrived backstage at the Barbican about halfway through the first half of Borge's performance. He peered at the backstage television monitors but the quality was not good enough to let him see the individual players. 'Which orchestra is playing?' he asked one of the backstage team. It wasn't my problem but, nonetheless, at that moment I fled!

Victor Borge's manager in the UK was Tito Burns, originally a musician who later turned to artist management. He was quite ferocious at first but I got to know him well and we got on fine. He generally insisted on providing the printed programmes for the performances so he could make something on the side. This was fine by me as they were undated and he clearly made money by supplying them at all Borge's UK dates. Then one year, I found him and his wife huddled in one of the dressing rooms at the Barbican during the afternoon sound check, busy with bottles of Tippex, a white, quick-drying liquid used to correct typed documents — I know, quite unimaginable now! They were carefully covering the previous year's touring dates which, unusually, were featured in the programmes he was providing. I really had to laugh; that gave a new meaning to 'chutzpah'.

I actually presented Victor Borge at all three major London concert halls. When he died on 23 December 2000, I went onstage before the afternoon Christmas concert I was presenting at the Barbican in front of a packed audience to say a few words in tribute to a great artist, a superb comedian but above all a truly wonderful man. They particularly loved the story about his encounter backstage with the Baroness. I rather think he would have liked that.

Of all the many artists I have worked with, he really was very special. A trained classical pianist, Borge was actually his first name. He fled on the last ship to leave Denmark for Sweden before the arrival of the Nazis, the Danes having evacuated all their Jewish population by this point. He travelled on to the USA where he adopted Victor as his first name. He soon found that audiences greatly appreciated his quips and asides which he introduced into his until then rather more serious concerts of classical music. So it became his act and brought him fame and wealth but did not change his immense kindness and generosity of spirit.

CHAPTER ELEVEN

ALL THAT JAZZ AND MORE

In 1980, I got the opportunity to promote jazz when my old friend in New York, Klaus Kolmar, suggested I might like to look at the Preservation Hall Jazz Band from New Orleans. They were already an institution back on their home territory and, from the pool of players based there, they regularly sent out tours throughout the United States and beyond. Anyone who has visited New Orleans will likely be aware of Preservation Hall, which first began in the 1950s, dedicated to supporting the unique jazz music of the city. The very name conjures up the image of traditional New Orleans jazz that gets feet tapping and everyone swinging. I put a small number of dates together including one at the Royal Festival Hall. Ticket sales in London were particularly good and by the time the band arrived, led by Allan Jaffe, the founder of Preservation Hall, the date was virtually full.

Then disaster struck – the trumpet player was taken ill. Allan seemed unfazed and announced they were flying in a replacement. Step forward Kid Thomas Valentine, an eighty-year-old legend in the jazz world. He gave a staggering performance and, when the concert was nearing the end, he and the other members of the band struck up 'When the Saints Go Marching In', the unofficial anthem of New Orleans. They moved out through the audience, gathering people to join them in a conga as they processioned round the auditorium. Then, all of a sudden, Kid Thomas appeared in the balcony leading more members of the audience in the conga. How he found his way up there, I will never know. At the end, the applause was prolonged and thunderous. We sold masses of records which we'd had specially imported as they were not available over here.

Two days later, a stern letter arrived from the South Bank reminding me that it was strictly against the rules to conga through the audience. I couldn't resist; I wrote back, prefacing my letter with a note that the following had to be sung to the tune of the Conga:

'We thank you for your letter, we will try to do better.

It was quite wrong to conga on ... '

I never heard any more about it. A few days after that, I had a letter from Buckingham Palace asking if Prince Philip could buy the records. Who expects the royal family to pay? Naturally, I sent him complimentary copies. After that, I brought the Preservation Hall Jazz Band back many times, including to the National Concert Hall in Dublin. The audiences there are always wonderful and they were enthralled from beginning to end. It helped that the former Irish Taoiseach Jack Lynch was in the audience and when the band serenaded him with 'Danny Boy' the crowd loved it, as did Jack Lynch, as indeed did I. You cannot be totally dispassionate as a promoter and sometimes it is good to let the emotion take a hold.

The Preservation Hall Jazz Band was not the only jazz I promoted. In 1990, I was offered the opportunity to present Miles Davis for a London gig, appearing at Hammersmith Odeon, as it was still then called. It was a bit of a coup and was away from my normal range of activities. Box office interest was substantial and I was able, after some tough negotiations with the artist's management, to negotiate an additional performance. Both shows sold out. Miles' youngest son, Erin, was on electric percussion and the set list began with 'Perfect Way'. I had the opportunity to meet Miles Davis and the other musicians in what turned out to be his final London appearances. Sadly, he died the following year.

Back at the Barbican in the 1980s, I presented notable performances by Ray Charles and his Orchestra and Lionel Hampton. Ray Charles had his own security detail with him who kept everyone including me away. At the end of the evening I was invited into his dressing room to meet the man himself. It was part and parcel of my job to meet and greet but, even so, I felt a great rush of pleasure when I shook his hand. He could truly be described as a legend. You know you are working with someone really great when the performance sells out way in advance and you suddenly get approaches from people you do not know, lying through their teeth, saying they so admire what you do and by the way could you possibly find me a pair of tickets for Ray Charles?

Film music programmes had become very popular and an evening conducted by Maurice Jarre was made even more memorable by the presence of David Lean himself in the audience. As the music of *Lawrence of Arabia* filled the auditorium, it felt really special to have not only the composer himself there, conducting his music, but also the director who had conceived and masterminded what is still, nearly sixty years on, one of the greatest films ever.

Ron Goodwin came to conduct his music, including for *633 Squadron*, *The Battle of Britain* and *Where Eagles Dare*. His off-the-cuff, cheery introductions went down very well with audiences and he was a really lovely man to deal with, always positive and sparky. He had written some really classic scores. He had replaced Sir William Walton in *The Battle of Britain* when the producers decided they need something more 'commercial' for the music, which was hard on the great composer of *Facade* and the score for Olivier's film of *Henry V*. In fact, it was Olivier, who played Air Marshall Portal in the film, who insisted that Walton's music be retained for a short section at the conclusion of the film, called 'Battle of the Air'. It is classic Walton and deeply moving but Ron Goodwin's 'Luftwaffe March' and the rest of his score really do fit so well with the film.

Henry Mancini with his music for the Pink Panther films and *Breakfast at Tiffany's* also came to conduct a programme of his music with the Royal Philharmonic and returned a year or two later in a double-header with James Galway where I had to add a matinee to the original Saturday evening show, such was the demand.

Another almost annual visitor at this time was Cab Calloway. He was forever associated with the Cotton Club in Harlem and audiences waited in anticipation for his 'hi-de-ho' moment, singing 'Minnie the Moocher'. He was already nearly eighty when I first met him but onstage he was a bundle of energy and it was always a pleasure to welcome him back.

Later on, I snapped up the chance of engaging Ute Lemper for a short season at the Queens Theatre on Shaftesbury Avenue soon after she had finished her season in *Chicago* at the Adelphi. *Life's a Swindle* was the title she used for her one-woman show, with just her and a pianist plus bass and drums and some very atmospheric lighting. The scene was set for a night in a Berlin cabaret with the wonderful songs of the Weimar era, which was brought to a shuddering halt by the rise of Hitler and the Nazis. 'A brilliant excavation of lost songs of raunchy old Berlin, as well as classics by Kurt Weill and Bertolt Brecht,' was how one critic accurately described the show.

In the late 1980s, I started working occasionally with BBC Radio 2. I would engage the BBC Concert Orchestra for a Saturday night Barbican or Royal Festival Hall concert, which would be broadcast live on the radio. I was invited for lunch to Radio 2's headquarters, then in Charlotte Street in Central London. 'Come at noon,' said my host, 'we can have a drink before lunch.'

His office contained an impressive-looking cabinet which he opened as I arrived, revealing a large selection of drinks. I opted for a gin and tonic, which he made into a large glass, filling it at least half with gin. We moved upstairs, me already walking very carefully, to where the dining room was situated. I was introduced to the head of Radio 2; there were half a dozen of us round the table and a very convivial lunch ensued accompanied by a liberal selection of fine wines; our glasses were constantly refilled. At the end of the lunch, as I was trying to say a coherent goodbye to the head of the station, my host interjected, 'Come back to the office and have one for the road.' I staggered after him and, as we got down to the floor level where his office was situated, a rather jolly fellow, rotund and glowing, was pushing a trolley laden with bottles. 'Ah,' he said to my host, 'do you need any refills?'

CHAPTER TWELVE

THAT'S CRICKET

The success of my concerts at the Barbican and the increasing number of dates being made available for me to fill led me to search for new ideas, always one of the most tremendously fun parts of the job. As I was putting together my first Christmas festival in 1983, I also had the December dates after Christmas to fill and I was anxious to come up with something for one of these afternoons which would appeal to a non-musical audience. Although the Barbican had been conceived as a concert venue, its size and layout provided flexibility for alternative types of performances that maybe would not fit quite so comfortably into other London concert venues.

Ian Maclay at the RPO suggested the perfect solution. He was a keen cricket enthusiast and had the bright idea of getting Brian Johnston to front a show about cricket. What could be more sensible, he argued, than a cricketing get-together in deepest mid-winter? Like so many others, I had known Brian Johnston's name almost for as long as I could remember. He was one of the reporters for *In Town Tonight*, which was one of the earliest television programmes I can recall seeing, and he was, of course, the doyen of cricket commentators.

I got in touch with Brian who was immediately attracted to the idea. He suggested a group of three panellists who would appear with him: E.W. Swanton, the legendary cricket reporter for the *Daily Telegraph*, and cricketers Tony Lewis and Tom Graveney. John Huntley provided some archive film and, so as not to forget altogether that we were staging the show in the Barbican, I invited my old friend Ian Wallace to sing a couple of appropriate numbers and to join in the general discussions. We titled our show very simply *That's Cricket* and added it to the programme.

I had decided to keep the tickets all at one price as I had no idea of how many people would want to come and with a single price we could fill from the stalls upwards. We tried to create an intimate atmosphere on the Barbican stage and put up some enlarged photographs of distinguished cricketers of yesteryear, including Jardine, Hobbs and Bradman. In the event, the hall was very nearly full and Brian, the music hall artist manqué that he was, did a solo opening warm-up of twenty minutes or so with the audience loving every moment of it. Each panellist was introduced in turn and this was followed by a short promotional film about the game from the 1950s. This led up to the tea break.

The second half passed off very well with the audience having an opportunity to ask questions, which were expertly fielded by Brian, knowing exactly to whom on the panel to pass them. By the end of the afternoon, we realised we had a successful formula for a show and Brian and I agreed to talk further after the holidays. Over a convivial lunch a few days later, we settled our plans and I went about booking a tour. Brian, meanwhile, decided that he would chop and change the panel, partly to bring in as many of his chums as possible and partly to ensure that he could thereby take account of the geographical location of each venue and provide at least one member appropriate to the area.

My agreement with Brian was that his fee would be net of all expenses, which in practical terms meant that I had to lay on the transport, meals and overnight accommodation wherever necessary. I discovered that 'Johnners', as we all learnt to call him, had a penchant for Muscadet and smoked salmon sandwiches. Mike Scoble, our production manager, hired a mini-bus with very comfortable airline-style seats. For the more distant venues involving overnight stops, we would set off in the mid to late morning. After half an hour or so, Johnners would suggest, 'Shall we break open the smokers and the Muscers?' A cry eagerly taken up by the rest of the team. I remember particularly on one occasion John Huntley saying as he munched away, 'You do these things so well, Raymond.' The bottles would flow, the sandwiches would be passed round and sometime later a smiling group of cricket lovers would arrive at their hotel, where some would take a little nap. In the backstage area, more Muscers and smokers would be laid out for pre-performance, interval and post-performance enjoyment.

Gradually, the number of team members who had taken part grew and we had a fantastic list of names to call on. Another planning lunch was called for with Johnners and Jim Laker, who had by then become a regular member of the panel. Halfway through, Johnners turned to Jim and said, 'Well, Gubbers says we ought to do so-and-so,' and I realised that I had become fully accepted as one of the cricketing fraternity. Such responsibility called on me to adjust to this way of talking but I confess I was bowled for six at Southend when Johnners arrived backstage and asked me, 'Have you seen Jenkers and the Gnome?' Jenkers, I should have guessed, was Christopher Martin-Jenkins, the cricketing commentator and writer but 'the Gnome' really had me stumped. It turned out to be the sobriquet for Keith Fletcher, Essex captain and later England's manager.

Brian's manner with the audience was easy and charming and they loved him. Early on at each performance, he would announce that he was wearing his Raymond Gubbay suit — 'small checks' he would add. His style was such that he could be almost as equally entertaining to people who knew almost nothing about cricket as for the real aficionados. I discovered that his choice of panellists was very carefully made; he avoided anyone who might prove controversial or who had views contrary to his own. He wanted the whole evening to move like clockwork and to leave the audience aglow from a combination of his charm and the real and infectious love of cricket that he passed on.

At St Albans, he invited Denis Compton as a special guest, not as a regular panellist, and so Compton had to wait for a greater part of the evening in the green room backstage, which was not too great a hardship as the customary smokers and Muscers as well as some red wine were all in place. The wine on this occasion was being dispensed in three-and-a-half-litre boxes and Dennis Compton set a new record for *That's Cricket*. He managed to get through a whole box on his own before going onstage but he still gave a sparkling and very lively performance, as befits one of the very few people to have played both cricket and football for England.

The Barbican performances continued more or less annually for the best part of ten years. Brian and I agreed that for the tenth anniversary we would do the performance in aid of the Lord's Taverners sports charity, which we both supported. Brian gathered together a really superb panel consisting of

Jonathan Agnew, David Gower and Henry Blofeld. Then, a few days before the performance, came the news that Brian had suffered a heart attack. We decided to carry on with the performance, turning it into a tribute to Brian who was still unconscious in hospital. Christopher Martin-Jenkins — Jenkers — kindly agreed to host the event. David Gower had somehow got his dates mixed up and told us that he would not be coming but Trevor Bailey, 'the Boil', who had been a member of the panel for so many performances, stepped in. The performance was deeply emotional but turned into the kind of celebration of both Brian and cricket that somehow felt appropriate at a sad and difficult time. At the end of the performance, I was able to present a substantial cheque onstage to Patrick Shervington of the Lord's Taverners. A few days later, the news came that Brian had passed away.

The last time I'd seen him had been a few months earlier when he asked me to join him and his wife Pauline for lunch at their home in St John's Wood. Their other guests were George Shearing, the blind English-born jazz pianist, and his wife. He turned out to be an old pal of Brian's and a great cricket enthusiast. The lunch was simple, according to Brian's rule — 'None of that foreign rubbish, just meat and two veg.' After lunch, we went into the garden where the roses were in flower and the sun was shining brightly. It was a perfect picture with Pauline and Johnners hand in hand showing us around. It is one I keep of him in my memory.

Brian Johnston was the archetypal Englishman and, although I deliberately never spoke politics with him, I sensed from his odd comment that he held trenchant views. He was a wonderful family man with a huge enthusiasm for cricket of course, but also music and the stage and for life itself. A war hero who had served in the Grenadier Guards and had been awarded the Military Cross, he was a true gentleman who never once said anything really unkind that I can recall about anyone. His memorial service at Westminster Abbey was oversubscribed many times over. His final act of service to the nation was being able to yank John Major, then prime minister, over to the memorial service and away from the political scene for a couple of hours; a couple of years would have been a real triumph but even a couple of hours was an achievement.

CHAPTER THIRTEEN

NOT QUITE KOSHER

The Barbican complex included two exhibition halls, originally planned to replace bombed-out warehousing on the site but later converted for exhibition use. It made sense, what with London's principal exhibition spaces located in west London and the Docklands regeneration a long way off, for the City to have exhibition facilities of its own. Talking to the people running the halls in early 1987, it was clear that there were many gaps in the exhibition halls' diary so I came up with the suggestion of mounting an antiques fair. They were receptive to this and I contacted Caroline Penman whom I did not know other than as the name behind the then twice-yearly prestigious and successful Chelsea Antiques Fair.

We met and she was very responsive to the idea, even though the dark, low-ceilinged, rather characterless exhibition halls themselves were nowhere near perfect for staging a fair of this kind. However, Caroline was highly experienced in this field and agreed that the City of London was a strong incentive for exhibitors, giving them access to City professionals on their own doorstep. We agreed to start with using just one of the halls which Caroline soon filled from her list of participating dealers at Chelsea and her other roster of fairs. All was set for the establishment of an antiques fair in the City of London. Then, almost out of the blue, Black Monday arrived on 19 October 1987, just a month before we were due to open.

The stock market crash was likened to Wall Street in 1929. Though not nearly as profound, it shook confidence and the mood changed overnight. But everything was in place for the fair and we carried on with our plans. I had booked fanfare trumpeters from one of the Guards Bands to herald the arrival of the Lord Mayor to open the fair. We were under way.

During the five days of the fair, business if not exactly brisk was certainly there for the taking for those with the right pieces at the right prices. There were some serious exchanges of money and we were encouraged by the feedback from exhibitors.

The following year, Caroline thought we should take on both halls with antiques in one and fine art in the other. She moved swiftly into action, eventually filling both halls in time for the autumn's event. In the meantime, our activities had come to the attention of Rob Mackenzie, head of exhibitions at EMAP, a big publishing group who, after the second year of the City of London Antiques and Fine Art Fair, made an offer to buy us out, which Caroline and I accepted. It had been for me a brief but interesting foray into the world of antiques, fine art and exhibitions, and one which I greatly enjoyed.

Meanwhile, my attention had been drawn to another type of exhibition, the Kosher Food Fair, which was a big success in New York. This brought together purveyors of all things kosher – food, beverages, wine and associated accessories for the kosher kitchen and household. After a visit to the fair in the US, I felt we might be able to mount something similar over here. I did, however, rather fail to acknowledge that there is a much bigger Jewish population in New York than there is in London.

I contacted the United Synagogue, who expressed interest in allowing their name to be associated with the fair to ensure, as I saw it, that everything was, well, kosher. Then things started to unravel. The graphic designer who I had engaged to design the brochure for exhibitors managed to produce a line drawing of a Menorah but with the wrong number of branches; I spotted this in time. What I failed to see was that he had misspelt the word 'synagogue' – quite how I missed this I do not know. Anyway, we had to do a complete reprint but really we needn't have bothered. When the brochures were at last posted out to likely exhibitors, the response was very slow. Those that did bother to get in touch, having been told the stand rate, would inevitably respond, 'Can't you do a deal?' It was one of those ideas which seemed so good at the time but which in the end dwindled away to nothing. I had to abandon any idea of getting involved with fairs and concentrate solely on my core business.

CHAPTER FOURTEEN

YEHUDI MENUHIN

Of all the artists I have worked with, probably none has given me so much pleasure as Yehudi Menuhin. My mother had heard him, as a child prodigy, practise in his room at the Hotel Adlon where he used to stay during his visits to Berlin in the 1920s, when she was governess to three of the proprietor's children. In the early 1980s, he was managed by Harold Holt Ltd, one of the more snobbish and unapproachable firms of artists' agents based in London. Even when I was fairly well-established, they still seemed unwilling to do any business with me; an enquiry I made at the time the Barbican opened was brushed aside in the usual brusque manner they seemed to employ. It was only after I got to know Eleanor Hope, who had originally been Menuhin's secretary and was then running Anglo-Swiss Artists, that I found a route through to Menuhin himself. We arranged a series of three concerts conducted by Yehudi Menuhin with the Royal Philharmonic Orchestra at the Barbican in the spring of 1984, each one featuring a young violinist suggested by Menuhin himself. I found an instant rapport with him and was delighted when he indicated that he would be very happy to do more work for me.

That autumn, Menuhin agreed to play the Bruch *Violin Concerto* with the London Philharmonic Orchestra. He was by now in his late sixties and had lost much of the delicacy of line which had been such a hallmark of his earlier performances. Yet there were still flashes of magic when the old Menuhin suddenly shone through, revealing a wonderful vignette of his former glory. After the concert, we all went to dinner and it was lovely to sit and relax with him, hearing him expound on so many different subjects. He had been among the first to visit post-War Germany and the former Nazi-occupied areas of Eastern Europe, bringing the magic of music and inspiring hope in the most troubled areas.

Soon afterwards, I accompanied him to Germany on part of his tour there. I joined him at Bremen where he was conducting and I was amazed to see how, after the concert, he was almost mobbed by a huge crowd which had gathered outside the hall to see him leave. In England he was respected and admired; in Germany he was idolised. His understanding and love for the people whom he never abandoned and always came back to was clearly recognised by them. We drove through the night to Hamburg arriving in the early hours of the following day. The reaction there was the same: absolute adulation from the huge crowd. Our next stop was to be Berlin.

I had never before visited Berlin. Of course the Berlin Wall was still firmly in place with glasnost still some years away and the city was effectively an isolated Western outpost behind the Iron Curtain. The Four Power agreement meant that only non-German aeroplanes could fly along the Berlin corridor, the designated flight path across East Germany. The planes had to descend to below ten thousand feet to prevent any onboard spy cameras being used to photograph large areas of the countryside.

Yehudi was conducting the Berlin Philharmonic Orchestra and I used the time when he was rehearsing to explore the city. My mother had told me many of the places which she remembered from growing up there. I went across to the East via the Friedrichstrasse crossing and had a cup of coffee in a café on the Unter den Linden. There wasn't really much to see in East Berlin except for rows of depressing looking apartment buildings, the radio tower and a lot of clapped-out Trabants.

Back in the West, I visited Checkpoint Charlie and climbed the watchtower to look across the wall to the East, which somehow underlined the strange contrast between the seemingly normal life in the West and deprivation and hardship in the East. Looking at the wall and the open space left in front of it, it was impossible not to feel both pity for and anger on behalf of the poor souls who had lost their lives trying to flee across it.

During our time there, a lunch had been arranged in Yehudi's honour by the local chamber of commerce and I found myself seated next to General Brooking, the General Officer Commanding of the British Sector in Berlin. It was fascinating to hear from him how the Four Power Agreement worked, with every plane needing to travel through the air corridor requiring written approval from the Soviets. He had a passion for music and sang, I discovered, in the Berlin Philharmonic Choir, his particularly tall frame making him very noticeable amongst the ranks of the choristers.

I worked with Yehudi on many more occasions, including several other concerts at the Barbican. I was even persuaded to see a staged performance of Handel's Messiah, which Yehudi was touring with the Polish Chamber Orchestra and a choir from the Baltic. I flew to Lille (this being before the opening of the Eurostar rail link) on a very rough flight from Stansted. The show was extraordinary. The four soloists were dressed in a mixture of costumes with one, I seem to recall, representing an angel. There was a pyramid on stage and members of the choir were robed and standing at the back. I think they clapped along during the Hallelujah chorus. It was quite a feat of endurance to sit through the performance. I couldn't understand how the great Yehudi Menuhin had become involved in this terribly misjudged production. Afterwards, choosing my words very carefully, I managed to avoid giving offence whilst at the same time offering no hint of any interest on my part for bringing this to London. It was a difficult tightrope.

Together with IMG, I organised Yehudi's eightieth birthday concert at the Royal Albert Hall, a joyous and happy occasion with many of his friends and colleagues present, including Anne Sophie-Mutter, who played a Mozart concerto. In December 1998, Yehudi conducted a Beethoven concert with the Philharmonia Orchestras as part of my Royal Albert Hall Christmas Festival. The *Symphony No. 8* made up the short first half. In the interval, Yehudi suddenly decided that he wanted to address the audience before the start of the *Symphony No. 9*.

The Royal Albert Hall had at that time no permanent sound system and so the only option was for him to use the emergency microphone always on standby in case the audience needed to be evacuated. So he emerged at the start of the second half carrying the microphone with the lead trailing behind him. He spoke, as only he could, sincerely and with deep conviction about Beethoven's *Symphony No. 9* and its relevance to the world around us and in particular the situation at the time in Kosovo. The audience was deeply moved; you could feel the atmosphere as he raised his baton at the start of the long journey towards the ultimate 'Ode to Joy'.

Afterwards, I went round to thank him. He was quite alone, no managers, no assistant, just him packing up his things as he had done thousands of times before. We spoke for a few moments and, before we parted, I said how much I was looking forward to the following year's concert we had arranged to mark the seventieth anniversary of his debut concert at the Royal Albert Hall. It was to be the last time that I saw him and, indeed, his last London concert. He died three months later.

So much has been written about Yehudi Menuhin both during his lifetime and after his death that there is not much I can add. He was a musician whose name and influence extended far beyond the world of music. He had incredible ideas and an enthusiasm and energy which even in his eighties seemed unabated. I will always feel it an enormous privilege that I had the opportunity of working with him on so many occasions.

The concert at the Royal Albert Hall in October 1999 that was to have marked the seventieth anniversary of his debut there turned out instead to be his memorial concert. It was a sad but brilliant occasion, commemorating his enormous contribution not only to music but to making the world a better place.

CHAPTER FIFTEEN

THE MUSIC OF ANDREW LLOYD WEBBER

I had worked often with Julian Lloyd Webber at the Barbican. He invariably performed the Elgar *Cello Concerto*, composed in the aftermath of the First World War, with great passion and commitment. His mother attended many of the performances and I got to know her quite well. I first met his brother, Andrew, when he and Julian appeared together in a charity concert at the Barbican.

I had often thought how interesting it might be to put together an evening of the music of Andrew Lloyd Webber. Then, by a strange coincidence, at the end of 1986 somebody introduced me to Mike Reed who was conducting the initial run of performances of *The Phantom of the Opera* at Her Majesty's Theatre. He saw no difficulty in putting together a suitable programme and suggested the 'Variations for Cello' as the centrepiece for the first half with a selection of show songs from *Cats*, *Evita*, *Tell Me on a Sunday* and *Phantom*. He also thought that he could persuade Sarah Brightman, then Andrew Lloyd Webber's second wife, to take part and he suggested a young singer who had been performing in *Les Miserables*, Michael Ball, to join her and share the vocal numbers. The programme was later altered to include some new material, including the song, 'Love Changes Everything' sung by Michael Ball, which was from Andrew's forthcoming musical, *Aspects of Love*, in which Michael starred. This was all very good news and I put together a couple of Barbican dates so that we could try out the programme.

What I had not reckoned with was that the great man himself would want to get heavily involved. Suddenly he announced that he was going to let us do the first performance of his new orchestral suite featuring music from *Evita*. However, this would necessitate an additional and unbudgeted rehearsal on top of the three already scheduled.

Andrew invited an eminent conductor to listen to the play through. 'What do you think?' he asked him when it was over. The conductor made some flattering noises and then proceeded to thumb through the score indicating two enormous cuts that he thought should be made. Andrew was visibly shaken but he had solicited the opinion and he was man enough to take it on the chin.

The performances at the Barbican went very well and, on the strength of these, we scheduled more at the Barbican and a short tour to major concert venues around the country. Andrew turned up at all of these, which in a way was very flattering but also quite nerve-wracking and exhausting. At Nottingham's Royal Concert Hall, he demanded that the sound desk be moved from its permanent position, which proved impossible. At Fairfield Halls, Croydon, he reduced the poor hall director to grovelling silence. He had told Andrew, very politely, that the performance was sold out and that it would be wonderful to welcome the show back again another time. Andrew's response was to tell him that the auditorium was far too small and that it would make absolutely no sense to bring the show back. The hall director just kept muttering, 'Yes, of course, too small, too small, I'm so sorry, we're too small.'

The real drama came when we got to Birmingham at the end of the tour. We were playing the NEC, Birmingham's exhibition centre, which had for our event an auditorium of eight thousand seats. It was something of an experiment on our part to see how the show would work in an arena. Andrew arrived before the rehearsal and suddenly decided that he wanted a bigger orchestra, even though the whole orchestra was being amplified and a very sophisticated sound system was in place. Eventually, I decided that I was better off away from the concert and so I decided to leave.

I walked outside to my car and got in, put the key in the ignition and started the engine. It was raining quite heavily and I was anticipating a slow drive back home along the M1. Suddenly, I was aware of two figures running across from the stage door. Mike Reed and Kathryn Enticott, who worked for Andrew, had clearly been deputed to talk me round to staying. Through the open window I told them that I was not upset, I was just rather fed up. Eventually, more out of sympathy with them having to stand in the rain, I said that I would come back inside. Andrew was waiting for me and embraced me warmly. The concert went very well and, at the end, Andrew went on stage to publicly thank everybody who had been involved in the tour. He reserved his biggest thanks for me as I squirmed in my seat.

CHAPTER SIXTEEN

THE GLC AND THE SOUTH BANK

I had been promoting at the South Bank since 1968, firstly at the newly opened Queen Elizabeth Hall and later at the Royal Festival Hall. The QEH, as it became known, and its smaller sister the Purcell Room were added to complement the Royal Festival Hall, which had originally been constructed in 1951 by the old LCC (London County Council) for the Festival of Britain. The LCC – who continued to run the hall – was superseded by the Greater London Council (GLC) in 1965. The GLC took a close interest in the running of the whole South Bank complex, particularly after Ken Livingstone took control of the Labour majority on the council in 1981. This continued until 1986, when the GLC was in turn abolished and the running of the centre was passed to the Arts Council.

It was always difficult to get dates at the RFH – the annual programme was formulaic with most dates being allocated automatically on a year-by-year basis in a comfortable, well-established routine. In fact, despite the changes to the organisation that superintended it, the system of running the venue had hardly changed since its opening in 1951, though it had been slightly ruffled by the decampment across the river by the LSO in 1982 when the Barbican finally opened its doors. In the early 1980s, symphony concerts made up the bulk of the programming at the Southbank Centre (as it became known in the 1980s), with the three London orchestras – the RPO, LPO and Philharmonia – taking the lion's share, and regular series from the BBC Symphony Orchestra, London Mozart Players, the Royal Philharmonic Society, regional orchestras and various choral and other groups. Jazz and light entertainment got the odd look in as did commercial promoters such as me.

In 1984, I found I was allocated, quite by chance, 14 February. It was very obvious what I should do with the date but it took me a while to work it out. Almost at the point when the diary copy had to be supplied to the hall, it struck me — a Valentine's Day concert with a red rose offered to every lady in the audience. The interest when the tickets went on sale was encouraging but received an enormous boost when Audrey Wise, chair of the Greater London Council's Women's Committee, announced very helpfully that it was racist and sexist to give out red roses. Quite what she meant was never clear. She seemed to have the idea that we should hand out hibiscus as this would be more politically correct. This dealt with, in her mind, the racial side but the sexist side was never properly explained by her. Was she suggesting we give out flowers to the men in the audience?

The media had a field day with news reports and special articles in the papers alongside radio interviews. Ms Wise gallantly conceded that she had scored an own goal by giving welcome publicity to my concert. It was my first experience of media spin, a lesson I was quick to take on board. Henceforth, Valentine's Day concerts continued as part of my annual programming in London and the regions.

In the same year, I mounted a production of *HMS Pinafore* at the Queen Elizabeth Hall for a short summer season. We had managed to get Frank Thornton — Captain Peacock from *Are You Being Served* — to play Sir Joseph Porter. Frank was a lovely man and threw himself with gusto into the role. All was fine during rehearsals and the final dress rehearsal went well. At the first performance, Frank as Sir Joseph entered accompanied by his ever-present sisters, cousins and aunts. Then came the patter number 'When I Was a Lad'. Frank dried, but completely. All you could hear was the plinkety plonk of the orchestral accompaniment and the chorus joining in the refrain at the end of each verse. The conductor was shouting out the words but it made no difference, Frank was silently mouthing bubbles whilst making ever frantic hand gestures.

By the final verse, sections of the audience were joining in. At the interval, I decided to give backstage a wide berth but, at the end of the performance, I thought I'd better go round and see him. I knocked tentatively on the dressing room door. Frank opened it, glass in hand. Behind him I could see his wife Beryl and a guest. I thanked him for his performance. 'Had a bit of a memory lapse,' he said, 'but I don't think anybody noticed.'

Just after the Valentine's Day business, strange goings on at the South Bank were reported. It seemed that the GLC, which still had responsibility for the complex, was suddenly starting to take a much deeper interest in it. The reason for the sudden in-depth look by the GLC was reported to have followed an incident on Thames Day, a council-organised cultural celebration, when Lawrence Peterkin, a senior GLC officer whose responsibilities included the London Fire Brigade, wanted to come inside to use the loo and was told that these facilities were not available to non-concert goers and, furthermore, even they could not gain admittance until one hour before the performance. Mr Peterkin asked to see the duty manager. Twenty-five minutes later the hapless functionary arrived, astonished at being summoned downstairs during the day — such a thing had never, ever happened before. Who was this person demanding his attendance? He very quickly found out and a few days later Mr Peterkin's portfolio at County Hall had been enlarged to include the South Bank alongside his other responsibilities.

Michael Kaye had come across to run the South Bank halls in 1980 after the turmoil of running the LSO prior to its move to the Barbican and had probably thought he was entering the quieter backwaters of Festival Hall. The poor man soon found his life changing rapidly. Mr Peterkin wanted to know why the hall was not open all day long. Why the refreshment areas could not be opened up to non-concert goers? The restaurant alone catered for non-concert goers, although its prices tended to put off all but the more affluent clientele. This 'open door' idea was totally alien to the South Bank, which had gone largely untroubled by new ideas since the Festival of Britain packed up in 1951.

Very soon, the hall was presenting a much more inviting image with facilities for both eating and drinking and free foyer entertainment too, all things which the Barbican had already successfully pioneered. For all the traumas involved in setting up the new image, it was all very positive and only marred later by the closing down on purely political grounds of the champagne bar which was regarded as representing quite the wrong image for a venue run by the left-leaning GLC.

I liked Lawrence Peterkin; he was bluff and honest and he got things done. Over lunch one day, we discussed the *HMS Pinafore* production which I had revised at his request for a short summer at the QEH. What, he wanted to know, could we follow it with? We examined the Gilbert and Sullivan canon and then an idea struck me. Why not, I suggested, take *Iolanthe* and update it into something more relevant to the current battle going on between Mrs Thatcher and the GLC? This struck a chord – he knew at once that if we got it right, it would certainly find favour with his political masters. So he asked me to develop the idea.

I dropped a note to Ned Sherrin, whom I had recently met when he came to see *Napoleon*, with its live orchestral accompaniment, at the Barbican. At the dinner interval between the two halves on the Saturday showing I had been introduced to him in the Barbican restaurant. It was Ned Sherrin who had moved the BBC forward in the early 1960s from its grovelling, deferential attitude to something much more immediate and cutting edge with *That Was the Week That Was*. It launched the career of David Frost and changed the face of television for ever. Would he, I asked in my letter, be interested in adapting *Iolanthe* and perhaps directing it?

His response was heavily qualified. He might be able to do the adaptation, although following Caryl Brahms's recent death he would have to find a new writing partner. He mentioned the name of Alistair Beaton as one possibility. He said, however, that he would not be able to direct it. Then a few days later, he suddenly became much more enthusiastic; he'd clearly spoken to Alistair and he had also decided that he might, after all, be able to direct the production. Alistair in fact became the driving force in the writing partnership, writing some of the show's most memorable and witty lines.

I persuaded Laurence Peterkin to underwrite the cost of commissioning the writing; he was nervous about definitely going ahead with the production until he had seen the script, an understandable precaution.

Some weeks later, Ned rang me to say that they would be finished the following week and so I set up a meeting with Peterkin, Ned and Alistair at the RFH for a read through. Ned and Alistair had changed the title to *The Ratepayers' Iolanthe*, which indicated the way they were heading. Ned played all the parts in a variety of accents and I laughed a great deal. At the end, Lawrence Peterkin turned to me and asked me what I thought. It was very clear that he did not want to give the first opinion. I felt no such constraints; I said I thought it was very funny and would make great entertainment. Lawrence agreed and we got the green light.

Iolanthe was the ideal vehicle to adapt to show the current impasse between Mrs Thatcher and her government on the one hand and the GLC led by Ken Livingstone. In the original, the House of Lords and the Lord Chancellor are at odds with the Queen of the Fairies and her cohorts who are supporting Strephon (who is only half a fairy as his mother married a mortal and was banished from fairyland). Of course, being Gilbert and Sullivan, it is a glorious send-up of the pomposity of the English upper classes. Among the best-known lines are those of Private Willis in the 'Sentry's Song', whilst musing on guard duty outside the Palace of Westminster, 'that every boy and every gal that's born into this world alive, is either a little Liberal or else a little Conservative'. The Lord Chancellor's 'Nightmare Song' is another *piece de resistance*. Ned and Alistair changed the Queen of the Fairies to Mrs Thatcher, the Lord Chancellor became the Chancellor of the Exchequer and young Strephon was renamed Red Strephon (Ken Livingstone), the leader of the GLC.

Ned's contacts were in full use with the casting. He had lots of ideas and put together a wonderful cast and a great artistic team. Daphne Dare produced a lovely stage design which placed the orchestra behind the set, thus allowing the action to be played right out into the audience. Ned's original choice to play the Lord Chancellor / Nigel Lawson role, Lance Percival, pulled out shortly before rehearsals started but Ned found a replacement almost immediately, Doug Fisher. He had played Richard O'Sullivan's mate in *Man about the House* but also made frequent television appearances in a variety of roles.

At first, I was a little worried. I realised that he had come late into the planning and therefore had had no time before rehearsals started to learn the part but he did not seem to be getting into it at all. The rest were doing wonderfully with Gaye Brown honing her Mrs Thatcher role to perfection and David Kernan getting more nasal by the day as 'Red Strephon'. Michael Robbins, whom I remembered from *On the Buses*, was doing the Private Willis role as an MI5 agent — 'When all night long I tap your phone, I do it to protect democracy.'

Rehearsals took place in a church hall in Pimlico and the daily routine would normally allow Ned to slip off to his nearby home leaving the choreographer, Lindsay Dolan, in charge. Then, as rehearsals were drawing to a close and we were about to move into the hall, the press got wind of what we were actually doing and various television news crews descended on the rehearsal hall. Suddenly, Ned was very much in evidence, strutting in front of the cameras, issuing instructions, 'Darlings, more of this please, less of that' and so on.

The move to the hall for final dress and technical rehearsals produced, as it so often does, a tightening up all round. The knowledge that the first night is only a matter of two or three days away tends to sharpen the mind and quicken the heartbeat. Everybody was beginning to pull out all the stops but the most remarkable of all was Doug Fisher.

Suddenly, in his Nigel Lawson wig and pinstripe suit he became the Chancellor (of the Exchequer in this production). He looked like Lawson, he acted like him and when, from his red budget case, he unpacked his sandwich lunch, he caught the mood of the man exactly. His 'Nightmare Song' was a triumph and his trio with David Firth and Dudley Stephens was to bring the house down at every performance — 'The dollar is up and so is the franc, cry the whole way to the bank.'

At the first performance, Ken Livingstone sat near the front and went on stage at the end to take a bow with his lookalike. The audience roared their approval and, over the following days, the press was excellent, business boomed and we were soon sold out for the entire run. Tory MPs were spotted arriving anonymously once the house lights went down, Kenneth Clarke amongst them.

It had been a really exhilarating experience from start to finish, watching the germ of an idea brought to fruition, working with a wonderful team and seeing a very successful result. I loved the opening night as it was the first time we had a reaction from a packed house. I found it was always difficult to take an objective view when putting together any kind of stage production. Watching the rehearsals over a period of weeks, I had felt we had something really good developing and once we were in the venue with dress rehearsals, I felt even more confident of this. In the end though, it is always down to the press and the public and I was delighted that both were very enthusiastic.

Suddenly, there was pressure for us to transfer the show to the West End. The GLC put up some of the money; I, perhaps foolishly, put up most of the balance as I really wanted to see the production in the West End and this seemed to be the only way. Then a problem arose which I had never anticipated. Equity, the actors' union, decided that three provisional members in the cast could not transfer with the show to the West End, which was at the time a closed shop for full union members only. We appealed to the London Theatre Council, which included representatives from Equity and the West End managers. It seemed to me ironic that we should be trying to get Equity to agree to help us move a production which was very much against the government of Mrs Thatcher when she was about to end their protected status as a trade union. One of Equity's representatives was the deeply unfunny character from *Are You Being Served*, Nicholas Smith, who played Mr Rumbold. His real-life persona made Mr Rumbold seem almost kind and sympathetic by comparison. We lost, of course, but Equity's gain was perhaps a Pyrrhic victory as a great deal of adverse publicity for them followed in the press and media.

Meanwhile, Stoll Moss Theatres, as they then were, were keen to offer us the Victoria Palace but then got cold feet about the political consequences, although why was never explained. Then I found we could go to the Phoenix Theatre on Charing Cross Road, never a first choice but it seemed as though it would be all right there. Of course, it was not all right, our 'strictly limited season' of twelve weeks was eventually cut in half. When we posted the closure notice at the theatre, the cast were deeply dejected. Many of them, I think, had thought that far from cutting the season, we would actually be able to extend it. The audience for the transfer just was not there. What had been funny and topical at the South Bank, where the prices were much lower, now seemed out of place in the more expensive West End. Ned Sherrin, however, won an Olivier Award.

The GLC had derived enormous publicity from *The Ratepayers' Iolanthe* and so Lawrence Peterkin invited me to propose something similar for the following year. Ned and Alistair came up with *The Metropolitan Mikado*, an adaptation of *The Mikado*, set some years hence when Great Britain had become a colony of Japan. Mrs Thatcher was back, this time with the formidable Louise Gold playing the Katisha / Mrs T part; Michael Heseltine / The Mikado was portrayed by Robert Meadmore with a Tarzan-like appearance and a flak jacket, and Martin Smith had the Ken Livingstone /

Nanki Poo part. The whole cast was tremendous and the show proved an enormous hit and successfully transferred from the Queen Elizabeth Hall after its three-week run to the adjoining and much bigger Royal Festival Hall for a further week. This time, however, the audience did not include Neil Kinnock and his family. They had come to *The Ratepayers' Iolanthe* and all loved it but surprisingly hadn't returned to see *The Metropolitan Mikado*, whose cast of characters included a Welsh windbag of remarkably similar appearance to Mr Kinnock.

The ongoing stand-off between Mrs Thatcher and her Conservative government and Ken Livingstone and the GLC had reached a crescendo and Mrs Thatcher had by now decreed the forthcoming demise of the GLC – it was to be abolished, the date of execution set for the following spring. Lawrence Peterkin invited us to do a final production in the dying days and Ned and Alistair came up with an idea for an original review to run for five days at the QEH. At the same time, I suggested a concert of excerpts from The Ratepayers' Iolanthe and The Metropolitan Mikado for a single performance at the RFH.

The GLC was fully underwriting both projects and I suddenly had a call from County Hall. Could I please arrange to go to room so-and-so at County Hall before four o'clock the following afternoon, which was when the government's new piece of legislation forbidding the GLC from handing out any money would come into effect. So I found myself in a queue outside the relevant room. As it snaked forward, I was aware of a lady at a desk recording information given to her by each person as they came to the head of the queue and then writing out a cheque. After the Hackney Lesbian and Gay Project and the South London Peace Campaign had had their cheques, it was my turn. 'Raymond Gubbay Limited,' I said. 'Ah yes, sign here please,' she said as she wrote out our reasonably substantial cheque.

The concert was a great success with a capacity audience renewing their acquaintance with Ned and Alistair's list of comic characters from their two adaptations. Afterwards, I went over to the QEH for the final performance of their review. When it was over, I met up with Malcolm Young, the South Bank's planning manager. Over at County Hall, we could see Ken Livingstone and his colleagues on a giant screen as they gave the eulogy for the passing of the GLC. Lawrence Peterken, meanwhile, had decamped for Scotland to run the Strathclyde Regional Health Authority, where he seemed to be particularly looking forward to addressing an outbreak of Legionnaire's disease.

But the Royal Festival Hall looked like a bomb had hit it, with rubbish and filth everywhere. In the auditorium, one of the hall's Steinways, its lid missing, was sitting at a precarious angle perilously close to the edge of the concert platform. The GLC had refused the Arts Council permission to safeguard and secure the building before midnight, which was the moment of the GLC's demise. It was a sad end to the GLC which had done so much for the arts in London in particular but it was even sadder that the GLC had cared so little for its crown jewels that it was prepared to see the Royal Festival Hall nearly destroyed in order to make its political point.

From March 1986, the South Bank was to be run by a board which was appointed by the Arts Council, which thus found itself funding one of its clients which happened to be itself. How on earth would the Arts Council be able to fairly police the activities of a part of itself in an impartial and fair manner? The question was never really answered and it was only later that the South Bank Board was set up as an entirely independent entity.

The senior team installed to run the complex comprised Richard Pulford, a career senior-grade civil servant who had been drafted in from the Treasury to be the administrative head, and Nicholas Snowman, who was to be the artistic director. I had known Nick Snowman for years as his uncle was a client and friend of my dad's. Nick had been up at Cambridge and was subsequently instrumental in co-founding the London Sinfonietta. Later, he moved to Paris to work with Pierre Boulez. His family ran the jewellery business Wartski and Co., and his father even appeared alongside Roger Moore in the scene in Octopussy when he accompanies James Bond to Sotheby's for the sale of a Fabergé egg.

A grandiose scheme was announced by the new team months before the end of the GLC's tenure had even ended. Terry Farrell, the architect, had devised a large-scale plan which involved putting an undulating roof over the entire site and adding in lots of retail space. This scheme like so many of its successors never got anywhere. It was nearly twenty years on before something was done to improve the RFH, which by now was very much in need of it.

.....

Snowman's well-known love for contemporary and avant-garde music soon influenced his planning. The South Bank would be a place where the venue itself would directly control much more of the programming. This may have made sound sense on paper but ignored entirely the realities of three London orchestras and various other organisations all wanting to continue controlling their own programming. Richard Pulford, whose health had in any case been suffering, parted company with the South Bank and Snowman was left in sole charge for several years.

I got into trouble with him early on when I suggested that the South Bank was going to repeat the South American Festival, which they had just staged, the following year. Only this time they would be flying the audience to South America as it would be cheaper. He was constantly carping on about my concerts and yet he had never actually been to one. I annoyed him again when I was quoted in the press as saying that you could no longer programme anything at the South Bank which had a tune you could hum. Then, one year when I was presenting a performance of *The Glory of Christmas* as part of our Christmas series at the Royal Festival Hall, he suddenly turned up with a large group of MPs.

The National Lottery, set up by John Major, had come into being and its first awards included a massive sum to fund the Royal Opera House's redevelopment. Snowman was lobbying at the time for lottery money to fund the latest redevelopment scheme at the South Bank and he presumably thought that this was a thoroughly safe concert to which to bring the MPs. He was wrong; I could not resist using the occasion to play a little joke on him. In the interval, I told the conductor that we were very honoured by this visit and as it was Snowman's birthday, could he please make a suitable announcement early on in the second half and get everybody to sing 'Happy Birthday', which he did. Never have I seen a man crumple so quickly. Snowman's attempted remonstration at least to those surrounding him was completely drowned out by the audience's rendition of his birthday greeting. My lasting image is of him sitting head down with dozens of MPs and other well-wishers slapping him on the back and shaking him by the hand. It was not his birthday, but nobody present knew that apart from him and me.

Soon afterwards, I co-promoted a recital by Montserrat Caballé with piano accompaniment at the Royal Festival Hall. It was sold out to such an extent that we had to add seats at the last minute on the concert platform in the area normally occupied by the orchestra. Caballé, true to form, had declared shortly before the start that she was not well and that if we wanted her to go on we would have to announce to the audience that she was only appearing under pressure from the management. This seemed unwise, so I had the relay system to the dressing rooms switched off. I then asked the duty house manager to make a simple announcement that Madam Caballé was unwell and craved the indulgence of the audience.

She emerged from her dressing room just before she was about to go on stage and asked if we had made the announcement. I said we had and she looked at me rather quizzically before moving onto the concert platform to start the recital. Later, she announced to the audience that she was not well but that next time she would make for them 'free concert'. Great cheers and applause greeted this news but I was dumbstruck. How to get out of this one? Next day, the box office manager rang to say that many people had been ringing to ask for the details of the free concert. 'Free?' I said. 'Did you say *free*? Madam Caballé said *three* concerts but as her accent is quite heavy, perhaps people did not understand her.' He swallowed it and told me later that people were very nice and understanding when he explained to them that they had misunderstood her.

CHAPTER SEVENTEEN

GILBERT AND SULLIVAN

The D'Oyly Carte Opera Company paid regular visits to Golders Green Hippodrome and, when I was a child in the early 1950s, I was taken to see *The Mikado* one Saturday afternoon. The company was then still very popular and had the monopoly of performing the works of Gilbert and Sullivan.

Richard D'Oyly Carte had brought the two of them together and, after the abortive debut with *Thespis* in 1871, D'Oyly Carte engaged them in 1875 to write a 'curtain-raiser' (a short piece to open the evening) before the main event, which was to be Offenbach's *La Périchole. Trial by Jury* was an enormous success, with Sullivan's brother, Fred, playing the Learned Judge. D'Oyly Carte spotted the potential of continuing the triumvirate, with Gilbert and Sullivan creating new works together which he would produce. For twelve years from 1877, one hit followed another, including *HMS Pinafore*, *The Pirates of Penzance* and *The Mikado*. Fred Sullivan died soon after *Trial by Jury* and so George Grossmith was engaged as the 'patter man', creating such wonderful characters as Sir Joseph Porter, the Major-General and Ko-Ko. He left the company before *The Gondoliers*, which was the last great success of Gilbert and Sullivan – although not in America where it was dubbed 'the gone dollars'. Two later works never really caught on, the old magic had somehow evaporated. In 1882, D'Oyly Carte opened his newly constructed Savoy Theatre alongside the Thames on the site of John of Gaunt's Palace of the Savoy. Later, from the profits of *The Mikado*, he was able to build the Savoy Hotel.

After my initial introduction to *The Mikado*, I went many times to the Hippodrome during the annual visits by D'Oyly Carte. They happened to be playing the theatre at a time when I was sitting my O Levels and I found it very relaxing before a heavy day of exams to watch a Gilbert and Sullivan production. It was a very useful path towards an appreciation of opera, also trodden, I have discovered, by so many others. By my late teens, I had tired of it and much preferred going to 'real' opera but I never really lost my enthusiasm for it, the silly topsy-turvy plots and the sometimes sublime but often banal music. And I have never been able to forget any of the words — they stick like glue.

The D'Oyly Carte Company, meanwhile, was grinding towards an ignominious end, which came in 1982 at the conclusion of their season at the Adelphi Theatre in London. I had taken a colleague to see *Pinafore* as he had never seen the company perform and I was intending to do a small-scale production of it at the Queen Elizabeth Hall the following summer. Neither of us could believe how low the standards had sunk.

Some years later, the company was revived as the New D'Oyly Carte Opera Company and achieved a good measure of success under the enterprising management of Dick Condon, a beguiling Irishman whom I had known when he had taken over the management of the Theatre Royal, Norwich. Sadly, he died before he could implement all his ideas. The company continued touring and introduced non-Gilbert and Sullivan works into their repertoire. Some of the many fans of the old D'Oyly Carte Company found their non-traditional approach too revolutionary but most people were deeply grateful that one hundred years of cobwebs had been blown away.

By the late 1990s, the new company had found the cost of touring without any Arts Council support to be prohibitive. Their chairman, Sir Michael Bishop, had been using his personal money to keep them afloat but he had decided that he could not continue in this way. It was then that I had an approach from their general manager, Ray Brown, previously a trumpet player and orchestral manager and incidentally married to Welsh soprano Elizabeth Vaughan. She was the first Butterfly I ever saw back in 1963 at Covent Garden when the Royal Opera House could mount productions with 'house' artists and tickets were affordable. He wanted to know whether I would put together a concert tour for them.

Whilst we debated the matter, I had an idea to put them on for a week at the Royal Festival Hall during the summer season. I met Sir Michael at the press conference organised by Peter Thompson to announce the one-week run of *The Mikado*. It was not a great production but it worked quite well and we decided to have another go the following year with *HMS Pinafore*. In the meantime, at very short notice, the Queen's Theatre on Shaftesbury Avenue became vacant for a short Christmas season and I managed to put *The Pirates of Penzance* together at six weeks' notice. We had to compromise over the size of the orchestra as the pit was very small and this drew some adverse criticism from the press but this was keeping the company going and most of the notices were excellent. I even managed, in spite of playing just three and a half weeks, to cover costs.

The presentation of *HMS Pinafore* at the RFH was altogether different from the previous year's *Mikado*. It had a really funny production by Martin Duncan with great sets by Tim Hatley. But it very nearly did not happen. I had agreed with D'Oyly Carte that we could not go on with me taking the entire risk of mounting these productions on my own and that I would have to continue on a joint basis with the risk being split fifty—fifty. We had signed the agreements and everything was set to go when I received a call from the company saying that Sir Michael did not want the season to proceed.

This was at the start of Holy Week and I found myself on Maundy Thursday, in the midst of the Easter traffic build up, driving north on the M1 to Donnington Hall, the headquarters of British Midland Airways, of which Michael Bishop was chairman. I discovered him hunched up by his desk in obvious pain. He was going to have an operation on his back. He told me in the nicest possible way that he would not allow the season to proceed. He was going to put the company into mothballs. I pointed out that we were already committed and the South Bank Diary covering the summer period had already been proofed and was even then being printed, all to no avail. So eventually I had no alternative but to offer to underwrite the season myself simply in order for it to continue. I certainly did not wish to upset my very good relationship with the South Bank who would have been very distressed if the season had been cancelled. I drove back to London relieved that I had saved the season but extremely upset that I had been put in that position. I felt that the D'Oyly Carte should have honoured the agreement we had previously concluded.

The performances at the Royal Festival Hall went very well and I realised the production could have a longer life in the West End, especially if I could get the company back to the Savoy Theatre. So I contacted Sir Stephen Waley-Cohen, who managed the Savoy and who expressed moderate enthusiasm for the idea. I have since discovered that no West End theatre manager likes to give anything approaching an unequivocal response regarding theatre availability. It is part of the mystique that dates may become available or not as the case may be but only when all other possibilities have been explored. No one wants his theatre to be occupied by a short run when the next big success might be available just around the corner.

On this occasion, all the pieces fell into shape and so, in February 2000, the D'Oyly Carte Opera Company returned to the Savoy Theatre after an absence of many years for a six-week, later extended to nine-week, run of *HMS Pinafore*. It was very well received and had the added advantage of opening at a time when Mike Leigh's film about Gilbert and Sullivan, *Topsy-Turvy*, had just opened to great critical acclaim.

Stephen Waley-Cohen was interested in developing the relationship with the D'Oyly Carte Opera and with me and so we decided to follow on a few months after *HMS Pinafore* with a new production of *The Mikado* and engaged Ian Judge to direct. His production was interesting and featured lovely designs by Tim Goodchild. I had not worked with Ian before although I had particularly admired his production of *The Flying Dutchman* at Covent Garden when it was originally presented without interval. He was not the easiest person to get on with but he had good ideas and knew how to create stimulating work.

One of the cast made me laugh when he told me that the old-stager previously with ENO who was playing the title role in *The Mikado* had the rest of the cast close to giggling when they all joined hands to take the curtain call. He made an inappropriate comment about a young lady in the third row and then, when they next moved forward for a further bow, he muttered about the place being packed and that 'bloody Gubbay' must be making a fortune. How little he knew about theatre finances!

The Mikado was followed by a stodgy revival of *The Pirates of Penzance* that lacked sparkle and did not show off the company at its best. After a gap, the company returned to the Savoy the following year with *Iolanthe* and *The Yeomen of the Guard*. I was surprised how well *Iolanthe* in particular was received, given that to me it looked as if half the opening scenery was missing. Sparse was how I would describe the set.

Stephen Waley-Cohen and I both made concerted efforts to encourage the company to look at booking some West End names to join them for each production but our efforts were nearly always in vain. The new company was heading very much in the direction of the old company, building up its own intractable tradition and a stock response to any innovative suggestions, that generally started off with, 'Well we've always done it this way.'

We decided to revive *The Mikado* and the company announced they were in serious discussions with comedian Jasper Carrott to play Ko-Ko. I was pleased to see the company take what I believed to be a definite step in the right direction. Jasper turned out to be an ideal company man, neither demanding nor expecting anything other than to fit in with the ensemble. However, it did not turn out to yield quite the results I had hoped for. The trouble was that instead of letting him develop the character of Ko-Ko with something of his own style, they insisted on shoehorning Jasper into their traditional mould and the result was mixed. A great opportunity had been missed, a chance to really show that the company was breaking the mould and could start to offer something different and exciting.

A revival of *HMS Pinafore* turned out to be a last throw of the dice. Sam Kelly reprised his interpretation of Sir Joseph Porter and a great company worked their way through a twelve-week Christmas and New Year season. Martin Duncan's production had lost none of its edge but the West End business was unexciting. I tried to suggest various ways to Michael Bishop to keep things going. I even managed to get Francesca Zambello to agree to direct a production of *The Gondoliers*, which she loves, fitting it in between her busy schedule at the Metropolitan Opera, the Bolshoi, the Paris Opera and Covent Garden. It would have been a coup for the company to work with her and a real artistic statement of intent but they decided that they could not take the risk. It became clear that *Pinafore* would probably be the end of the company at least in its present form.

A few weeks after the season closed, I noticed an advertisement in *The Stage* announcing the sale of the company's store of scenery and costumes. They retained some of the historical ones in their care but everything else was going to be disposed of. I was sad that my efforts to keep the company going should have ended in this way. I had fond childhood memories of visits to see the historic company but in the end a promoter has to accept the inevitable. Not everything can be successful and a good promoter knows when to say 'enough'. I have always believed that in the end you shut the stage door behind you and move on to the next thing.

A few years later, I presented a short season of three of the Savoy Operas at the Gielgud Theatre on Shaftesbury Avenue. The Carl Rosa Opera Company, originally formed in late Victorian times and mothballed in 1958, had been resurrected by the enigmatic and energetic Peter Molloy. He had enjoyed success around the touring circuit and had also rather enterprisingly taken the company abroad. In 2008, with the help of Mig Kimpton, a veritable multi-talented florist-cum-theatre entrepreneur, he had put together some star performers for the five-week season. Alistair McGowan, the impressionist, had an excellent voice and towering presence playing the title role as the Mikado. In *The Pirates of Penzance*, Jo Brand in true operatic tradition played the Sergeant of Police *en travesti* with a performance that suited her solo, ending with its famous line, 'A policeman's lot is not a happy one.' Both she and Alistair were real team players, fully at ease and utterly charming with the rest of the company.

The biggest surprise of all was in *Iolanthe*. Peter and Mig had somehow managed to persuade the prima donna, Maria Ewing, to play the Queen of the Fairies. An operatic star with major appearances to her credit, I wondered how on earth she had been persuaded to join our motley band. Formerly married to Sir Peter Hall and mother of the actress Rebecca Hall, she too was absolutely at ease with everyone in the company and produced a lovely, rounded performance. The lines of her adversary, the Lord Chancellor, come back to me as I remember her,

> *It seems that she's a Fairy*
> *From Anderson's library,*
> *And I took her for the proprietor of a ladies' seminary.*

Towards the end of the week of performances of *Iolanthe*, Sir Peter Hall and some of the Glyndebourne crowd came to see the performance. I knew Peter and was so pleased to see him there but the whole evening had a

Right: *1985. With Victor Borge, originally a classically trained pianist who fled Denmark ahead of the Nazi invasion and turned himself into a brilliant comedian as well as being a great musician.*

Left: *With Henry Mancini, Mr Pink Panther himself, in 1986 after a concert he conducted of his film music. Michael Emerson is on the left.*

Below: *With New Zealand soprano Kiri te Kanawa and composer and conductor Carl Davis after a Barbican gala, 1984.*

Those early days following the Barbican's opening in 1982 were extraordinary. I had a tremendous amount of fun putting on all sorts of shows, which often sold out. Here is a selection of pages from the concert programme celebrating the centre's first five years, including: Victor Borge, the Yeomen of the Guard, Henry Cooper, Kings College Choir, Aled Jones and the Teddy Bears Concert with Michael Bond holding Paddington Bear. Jim Laker, Brian Johnston, Timothy West, Ian Wallace, Howard Blake, Ian Lavender and James Judd all appeared in the Christmas Festival. Also, Yehudi Menuhin, John Williams and the Johann Strauss Gala, Jimmy Galway and Henry Mancini duetting on flutes and, of course, Pavarotti taking his Masterclass.

All photos: Clive Totman

Right: *The first night of* La Bohème *at the Royal Albert Hall in 1996. I am next to Diana and Conrad Black and Barbara Amiel are to my right. We are all looking very formal but in fact Diana was so easy to talk to.*

Left: *The gala night for* Swan Lake *with English National Ballet, June 1997, one of Diana's last engagements before her tragic death a few weeks later. She's speaking to me and Patrick Deuchar, the Royal Albert Hall's chief executive.*

Below: *1996. This photo made the front page of* The Times *and helped sell out the season. As patron of English National Ballet, Diana always helped them in any way she could. ITV news managed to do an impromptu interview in the Royal Box which caused waves at the Palace.*

Above: *Another full house at the Royal Albert Hall. It always gave me a real thrill to see it completely packed out. The near-empty hall during rehearsals also has a very special atmosphere.* Photo: Phil Dent

Above: *Francesca Zambello's production of* La Bohème *in 2004 with sets by Peter J Davidson and costumes by Sue Wilmington. As Act I ended, the scene exploded straight into Act II with waiters on roller skates at the Café Momus and the demi-monde of Paris filling the stage.*

Right: *The music box presented to me by the Royal Albert Hall to mark the hundredth performance of Classical Spectacular in 1998. It plays 'Rule Britannia' — what else!*

Above: *The last act of David Freeman's production of* Carmen, *2003. We once lost our by then voiceless Don Jose at the end of Act I and another time Carmen herself succumbed in Act II but we managed to pull through each time.*

Below: *David Freeman's stunning 1998 production of* Madam Butterfly *with the David Rodger-designed Japanese water garden which emptied during the interval.*

From top: The King and I *at the Royal Albert Hall, 2008. It looked sumptuous but musicals proved a harder sell at the Hall.*

Derek Dean filled the stage with spectacular effects for this production of Romeo and Juliet *with English National Ballet.*

Carlos Acosta and Tamara Rojo in the tomb scene in the second revival of Romeo and Juliet *in 2014.*

Right: *The Church of England Conclave of Bishops paid a visit to Classical Spectacular. The Archbishop of Canterbury is with Patrick Deuchar on the right. Peeping out behind the archbishop is Desmond Tutu. I was thrilled to meet him.*

Below: *Miles Davis sold out two performances at the then Odeon, Hammersmith in 1998. It was the only time I presented at Hammersmith but boy, was it special.*

Right: *Ute Lemper beautifully recreated the atmosphere of a Berlin cabaret with the wonderful songs of the Weimar era at the Queen's Theatre.*

Left: *The Barbican was ideally suited to Preservation Hall Jazz Band. Just a beautifully dreamy evening of New Orleans jazz — what could be nicer?*

Clive Totman

Clockwise from above: *With Jo — the grandmother of my grandchildren, as I like to call her. She was responsible for the title of this book and much else besides; with Australian Royal Albert Hall CEO Craig Hassall at Anzac Cove, 2019; my two eldest grandchildren, Jessica and Ben, before the fiftieth anniversary reception organised by the Southbank to celebrate my five decades promoting there; with my six grandchildren, Emily, Jack, Ben, Ella, Joshua and Jessica, the dedicatees of this book. We're on a cruise along the River Thames with family, friends and colleagues in 2011 to mark my sixty-fifth birthday*

rather unreal feeling about it.

My last foray into Gilbert and Sullivan was in 2011 when I organised a gala at Cadogan Hall in memory of Philip Langridge who had died the previous year. He had appeared in that very first concert I had put on under my own name at the Theatre Royal in Bury St Edmunds, a Gilbert and Sullivan evening on 21 October 1966. His family was very supportive and agreed that the proceeds should be given to the mentoring scheme in Philip's name being run by the Royal Philharmonic Society.

I knew that Timothy West had a penchant for Gilbert and Sullivan and he readily agreed to compere the event. I also managed to persuade about twenty singers to come and perform their favourite number from the Savoy Operas. Sir John Tomlinson sang the 'Sentry's Song' from *Iolanthe*, Dame Felicity Palmer sang 'Katisha' from *The Mikado* and Richard Suart was of course Ko-Ko with his little list. Lesley Garrett, Timothy Robinson, Rebecca Bottone and her father Bonaventura and host of other singers provided a programme which took me right back to my roots. Philip's two daughters played in the orchestra and Ann Murray, his widow, and their son Jonathan were in the audience. Philip's son Stephen even managed to locate a couple of 1960s recordings of Philip singing Gilbert and Sullivan on the BBC. Hearing his voice again, as I had remembered it from all those years ago, was deeply moving.

We ended the concert with the quartet 'A Regular Royal Queen' followed by the entire ensemble singing the 'Finale' to Act II of *The Gondoliers*. The hall was packed as so many friends and colleagues had bought tickets and I was quite overwhelmed at the interval by friendly faces all having a great time. In the end, the concert raised close to £40,000 and I was so delighted to have been able to organise something in Philip's memory, a thank you for his support to me in my early days as a promoter.

CHAPTER EIGHTEEN

WORKING WITH THE ROYAL OPERA

S ometime in the late 1980s, Paul Findlay, a contemporary of my elder brother at school and by then in charge of the Royal Opera Company, contacted me to see whether I might be interested in booking the Royal Opera House chorus for some of my concerts. A refurbishment of the Royal Opera House had been 'imminent' for some years by this point (it eventually materialised in the late 1990s with the aid of funds from the newly established National Lottery) and I asked Paul what the plans were during the closure period. So began an interesting dialogue, as a result of which we began to look at an idea I had to present the Royal Opera to a much wider audience than existed at the ROH itself.

Arena opera had already been seen in London with mixed results but the production of *Carmen* at Earl's Court had been well received. I thought that the ROH would bring quality and Paul thought they would benefit hugely from appearing before a different audience. After some debate, we focused on Puccini's *Turandot*. The recent football World Cup had established 'Nessun Dorma', sung by Pavarotti, as very much the world's best known operatic aria and we thought that this would help us enormously in marketing the opera to a much wider audience than traditionally attended performances at Covent Garden. The ROH's production by Andre Serban was then six years old and had an exciting set that Paul reckoned could be adapted for an arena.

We decided to look at Wembley Arena as it was smaller than Earl's Court but we could still configure it so that there was seating for eight thousand

and a large thrust stage extending well into the auditorium and surrounded on three sides by the audience. Roger Edwards was in charge of the venues at Wembley – I had known him previously when he was running the Hexagon at Reading. I approached him and he was very keen to encourage the Royal Opera to come to Wembley.

However, soon after we signed the contract, Roger was summoned by Sir Brian Wolfson, the CEO of the Wembley Stadium complex. 'What is this about the Royal Opera supposed to be coming here?' Roger confirmed that this was true. 'Are you sure it is *the* Royal Opera? My friend ******* has called me to say it's some cheap jack outfit from abroad misusing the name.'

The friend who had apparently supplied him with this 'information' was a very well-known pop promoter who fancied himself as an opera buff as well. Roger was able to produce chapter and verse from the Royal Opera House itself as they had of course been involved in my negotiations with Wembley. It seemed that Victor Hochhauser wasn't the only one trying to do me down; more of my colleagues were keen to see this fail before it had even begun.

I had developed what turned out to be a short-lived business association with EMAP, which was then a large publishing company with an interest in exhibitions. They enlisted the *Daily Telegraph*, with whom they had a joint company, to support the production of *Turandot*. Meanwhile, the Royal Opera – which was being paid a straight fee and thus had no financial stake in the outcome – was busy adapting the production for an arena setting. Sally Jacobs, who had done the original designs, produced magnificent plans for adapting these to the much larger three-dimensional space which the thrust stage at Wembley offered. During negotiations, a point arose concerning complimentary tickets for the ROH staff. 'We normally do this,' said the ROH representative, 'and we would like it written into our agreement.' 'How many tickets are involved?' I asked. 'Well, there are 800 employees at the ROH so 1,600 tickets should cover it.' That was yet another clause that I managed to excise.

All this was being done at comparatively short notice and by May 1991 we were ready to announce the ten-performance run at Wembley, from December to January that year. The Opera House redevelopment had been further delayed and so our season would be running whilst the ROH itself was still open. For these ten performances, the ROH was assembling a magnificent company, including Gwyneth Jones, Eva Marton and Grace Bumbry amongst the five Turandots and an impressive list of six tenors to share the role of Calaf. Because the run was spread over consecutive days, with matinees too, and due to the casting being done at relatively short notice, it was necessary to have a roster of singers to alternate the parts.

Initial press interest was high but ticket sales were sluggish, despite the introduction by Wembley of an 0800 information line – then very much a new innovation. On the day that bookings opened, full of enthusiasm, I rang it. I was surprised to be greeted with a soothing female voice announcing, 'Ladies, are you having trouble with your orgasm?' Alarmed, I rang Wembley and they asked me to try again in half an hour. I did so, to hear the same smooth, sexy, female voice announce, 'Welcome to the *Turandot* information line ... ' Clearly Wembley used a very versatile provider for this service.

In the late summer, we introduced weekly meetings at the ROH to review progress over morning coffee. We assembled in the board room and our wide-ranging discussions always included an update on ticket sales. The ROH Trust had a special offer for its supporters which included not only top-priced tickets but also dinner in Wembley's own restaurant. How, I asked, were these selling? Flavia, the gracious administrator for the trust, coughed to clear her throat. 'Not very well, as yet,' she replied. Pressed by Peter Thompson, our press representative, to be a little more specific, she admitted that only two tickets had been sold for this particular scheme. It rather underlined the lack of interest in the Wembley project by the ROH's core supporters. We tried a number of interesting marketing initiatives and the number of tickets sold gradually rose so that a potential disaster in terms of ticket sales was turning into just a disappointing one.

One of our more enterprising efforts caused deep shock at the Opera House. We needed to find an actor to play the executioner who was to appear bare-chested carrying a large sword during one of the big moments in the first act. So we placed an advertisement in The Stage announcing an open audition at Covent Garden the following week and we made it clear that we were an equal opportunities employer, preferring not to use the waiver available for theatrical productions under the Sex Discrimination Act. In order to ensure good publicity, we engaged a roly-poly lady to join the audition queue of hopefuls. Peter had already tipped off the press that we would be auditioning any ladies who turned up even if it meant having a bare-breasted female executioner. Press interest was huge with lots of cameramen and reporters arriving to see the auditions taking place.

Our lady attracted a lot of interest with press speculation rife the next day as to whether the Royal Opera House really would allow us to engage a topless lady executioner. In the end, of course, we settled for an out-of-work body builder from South Wales but the whole exercise had certainly made an impression. When Neil Kinnock, then still leader of the opposition, came to see the show, he remarked on our choosing the Welsh candidate and asked why we had not gone ahead with our topless lady. I even managed to get a story in the press saying that we were going to place a giant clock within the set showing the countdown to 'Nessun Dorma'. It was all a joke but some retired colonel wrote complaining to the press that this was a disgraceful idea.

We were due to open in late December and rehearsals began some weeks earlier. I called in at the giant studio situated under Westway, the elevated section of the A40 heading out of central London, where the ROH was rehearsing. The opera was being restaged by Jeremy Sutcliffe, the staff producer who did a fantastic job in moving the production from its conventional proscenium setting into the much larger arena space at Wembley.

I knew quite a lot of the Royal Opera House chorus and staff and so got chatting to some of them during the rehearsal break. They were surprised to see me there as they said that the management from the Opera House never visited rehearsals. I do not know how true that was but I always made a point of dropping in on rehearsals; it was just the natural thing to do. Not only did it show my interest but it also kept me abreast of any intrigues and developing issues. This was never much of a problem but I like to think my presence from time to time allowed anyone who wanted to raise issues directly with me and I could forestall anything more serious from developing.

Many of the international soloists just turned up for the performances and were given a 'walk through' on the stage on the afternoon of the performance. Gwyneth Jones had two different Calafs for her two performances and the second one had virtually no rehearsal at all. During the riddle scene, he took up an entirely wrong position for the first question. So Gwyneth fixed him with a steely look and pointed out for him the route he had to follow in order to be in the right position for the second riddle.

Press activity increased as we got closer to the opening night and Richard Morrison from *The Times* arranged to do an interview with Jeremy Isaacs, general director of the Royal Opera House, and me at the Opera House. By now, rather late in the day, Jeremy had started to realise that there was a lot of publicity being generated by the Wembley season. As always, when I am being interviewed, I try to give an honest response to the question, albeit slanted in the direction I want to follow and with a certain edge to give focus. Nobody is keen to publish bland responses. So I was perfectly frank in response to Richard's questions about seat prices and how they compared with those at the ROH but Jeremy was keen to avoid any such comparisons. It made for an interesting piece when it was published a few days later with an accompanying photograph of Jeremy and me showing the very essence of bonhomie.

Amongst the many interviews I gave was one with Derek Jameson, a former editor of the *News of the World* and now a regular host on BBC Radio 2. Seemingly filled with good humour, he gave me a nice build up and then, turning to me, said, 'So tell me, Raymond, how are ticket sales?' This was going straight for the jugular, he obviously had inside information, but I didn't flinch. I abandoned my policy of giving an honest answer, looked him straight in the eye and lied through my teeth.

Very late in the day, once we had set up everything at Wembley, we realised that some of the seating was rather less comfortable than in the main body of the auditorium. So we hired several hundred cushions and Paul Findlay's son, Anthony, was employed to move them around according to which seats had been sold in these areas. Dress rehearsals had gone very well and a buzz was going round that this was going to be rather special.

The prime minister, John Major, was coming to the opening performance and Jeremy Isaacs arrived early, insisting on doling out champagne to my colleagues and me. Wembley's foyers were buzzing and there was a certain sense of excitement which I have only ever experienced at first nights, and particularly those involving a journey into the unknown. The smell of hot dogs and French fries mingled not unhappily with the more traditional operatic fare of champagne and smoked salmon sandwiches. In a sense, this echoed the mixture of the audience – an eclectic bunch ranging from obvious invitees who frequent most first nights to groups and families who had clearly never been to an opera before.

John Major, facing his first general election sometime during the following months, was keen to project an image as a man of the people joining in 'bringing opera to the masses' (which rather patronising phrase was never one I liked to use to refer to arena opera). He was photographed holding the programme with the title clearly showing, which was published the following day in various national papers.

The opening performance went very well. Staging *Turandot* at Wembley had taken a mighty effort from all quarters and the feeling of exhilaration and relief when that opening performance ended was palpable. Afterwards, the company and guests assembled for the post-performance reception. The PM, with his opera-loving wife, Norma, and various aides and bodyguards, arrived and we all settled down to unwind and relax. Following the meal, when he was about to take coffee, he noticed his wife getting agitated, 'Oh no, I won't have any, Norma wants to go,' he said and trailed off behind her.

Ted Downes, Sir Edward Downes, conducted most of the performances with enormous enthusiasm and commitment. Of the six Calafs, only one was able to bring the house down with 'Nessun Dorma' as Ted inevitably hurried on with the music leaving no time for applause. Dear Dennis O'Neil, with whom I'd worked many times at the Barbican, wasn't going to be daunted by this. He finished with his right foot raised up on the prompt box, which was protruding just above the front centre of the stage, and flung his arms out wide. The effect was immediate and even Ted had to allow a good few seconds for the applause before moving on.

The *Evening Standard* review, the first to appear, was very enthusiastic and the rest of the dailies followed in much the same vein the following morning. The Sundays were also pretty good. The one issue which nobody seemed too concerned about was the amplification, which in hindsight seems odd, given the amount of stick subsequently meted out to me on this very matter when I started producing opera at the Royal Albert Hall a few years later.

I enjoyed the season very much and watched all ten performances from the front. Business for the later performances started to pick up and queues formed outside the extended Portacabin which served as Wembley's booking office. But it was all rather too late; the ROH had enjoyed spending our money and the losses were substantial.

Both EMAP and the *Daily Telegraph*, our partners in this venture, were fully aware of the risk involved in going to Wembley and also how the bookings were going, so the end result would have come as no surprise. Nonetheless, I had to report the losses at the next scheduled meeting. 'There's good news and bad news,' I said. 'The good news is we have lost under £1 million; the bad news is but not by very much.' I don't think they appreciated my sense of humour. I discovered afterwards that one of the EMAP executive directors, who had insisted on being photographed alongside John Major on the opening night, used to boast about it being the most expensive photograph ever. 'That photograph,' he would say, 'cost me £1 million,' neatly forgetting that the *Telegraph* had stumped up half of this and that with tax write-offs and other balance sheet sleights of hand, the actual loss to both parties was much, much less.

But, as always, some good comes out of every situation. The production had been hailed as a great success in all other ways. With such a dire financial result I inevitably parted ways with EMAP. In addition, I had learnt a few lessons about staging arena opera.

In the Royal Opera House's annual report covering the year we presented *Turandot*, the Wembley project barely merited a mention. In fact, the chairman's statement managed to omit any comment about it altogether. I had succeeded in getting Covent Garden away from its rarefied and forbidding base into a more accessible venue and to present itself to a much wider public than it ever played to on its home territory. The project had attracted widespread attention, had been generally very well received and had given the ROH a real opportunity to show its critics that it could embrace ground-breaking changes. The audience across the run totalled well over sixty thousand people (the Royal Opera House can accommodate around 2,200 per performance). Not as many as we could have had but a very solid start. I wanted very much to continue building on the spadework we had all put in to get *Turandot* on at Wembley. It seemed to me that with less extravagant working practices, better budgeting, more time to plan, the

Royal Opera sharing the element of risk rather than having to underwrite the whole cost and, finally, another popular opera like *La Bohème* or *Carmen* the concept of arena opera could be developed even further.

I was not, of course, and would never dream of advocating this as an alternative to the Royal Opera's core activity but merely a way of attracting new audiences. But, whatever the profit and loss sheet recorded, *Turandot* at Wembley had allowed the Royal Opera to momentarily move itself away from the stilted world of the nineteenth century opera house for the first time. Placing an opera in a large setting – in this case one better known for football than for anything else – where tickets were affordable to many more people to my mind sends a clear signal that opera is for anyone who is interested in experiencing it. Unfortunately, so many years later, the Royal Opera is still stuck in the groove where maintaining a traditional horseshoe-shaped auditorium with its impractical sightlines is more important than going out and finding new audiences.

CHAPTER NINETEEN

BACK TO THE ROYAL ALBERT HALL

After I started on my own in 1966, I had no dealings with the Royal Albert Hall for several years. Though he had not begun them — they were a well-established tradition going back long before the war — Victor Hochhauser managed for many years to maintain almost a complete monopoly on the Sunday night concerts there.

At that time, the hall maintained a secretary and lettings manager, a hangover from the Victorian era, the formidable Marion Herrod, who seemed to exert as much if not more power than the hall's director. Any applications for dates had to pass her scrutiny. Miss Herrod was responsible for keeping most rock and pop groups away during her tenure as she considered them unsuitable for the Royal Albert Hall. She famously questioned whether a concert by Mott the Hoople, a well-known rock group from the early 1970s, might cause a riot. She managed to hold onto her position until soon after the Barbican opened. Then something occurred and suddenly she was gone, having been a permanent part of the establishment there for what seemed like an eternity. I heard later that she had applied for a job at Croydon's Fairfield Hall but after that, she simply disappeared. Unsurprisingly, the post of secretary and lettings manager was abolished and the hall's director at last assumed overall control.

At the time, the director was Cameron McNichol, a seemingly rather dour Scotsman who had served as deputy director before being appointed to the top job. I had been promoting at the hall since the early 1970s, partly thanks to the kindness of Robert Patterson, who was very helpful in opening the doors for me, when I staged my first shows there in 1974. Then, the opening of the Barbican in 1982 and all the exciting opportunities that offered to promote on a grand scale in London meant I'd had little to do with the RAH for a number of years. However, I kept in touch and I wanted to try out another idea which had been in my mind for a long time. Putting together a programme of popular classics was something that I was doing all the time but suppose it could all be done on a more spectacular scale? Getting beyond the traditional concert audience was a challenge which I think I had achieved in the early days of the Barbican. Now I wanted to take it to the next stage.

So I booked a single date in October 1989 and put together a programme of twenty or so 'orchestral lollipops' (the rather dismissive term given in some quarters to classical favourites), ending with the *1812 Overture*. I engaged the Royal Philharmonic Orchestra, a couple of Guards Bands and historical re-enactment society the Sealed Knot to fire off their muskets in the 1812. Thus, *Classical Spectacular* was born. I added the epithet 'classic after classic after classic', booked ads in the press and the concert was sold out in a few days, so I scheduled a matinee as well which also sold out very quickly. Realising I had hit on a winning formula, I added more dates the following January and so on, with the eventual and enduring two seasons a year emerging with spring and autumn dates. A couple of years on, lasers were added giving rise to the tagline, 'music, lights, lasers'.

When the Sealed Knot no longer wanted to continue their association, a group of their former adherents was happy to be engaged under the title of the 'Moscow Militia', a name I invented. I recalled that when Napoleon eventually reached Moscow in 1812, he found it deserted and in flames. During his long march back west with an army of ever-depleted numbers, he was harried by Russian irregulars whom I imagined might have included elements of the Moscow Militia. Well, that was my reasoning to myself. Although I no longer have anything to do with the concerts, I am still very proud that *Classical Spectacular* continues to this day.

In the same year as the first *Classical Spectacular*, Cameron McNichol moved away to take up the position of running the new Royal Concert Hall in Glasgow. The hall appointed Patrick Deuchar, who had previously run the World Tennis Association, as chief executive. I liked him immensely as he had a lot of enterprise and drive and he pushed the hall forward into a number of new areas where it had never previously gone.

Though that was certainly not the last I saw of Cameron. A year or so after he moved to Scotland, he called me to ask whether I would join him the following Wednesday for the Scottish Businessman of the Year Award lunch which was going to take place aboard HMS *Ark Royal* at Leith harbour. It seemed such an outrageous idea that I agreed and found myself the next week on an early flight to Edinburgh, as the celebrations were due to start at 11.30am. On the dockside, I discovered Cameron waiting ready with my invitation; we mounted the gangplank and joined an already substantial crowd on the flight deck.

I had never been on an aircraft carrier so this was a novel experience. On the quay, the band of the Royal Marines from Rosyth was marching up and down playing selections of light music and show tunes whilst a brace of helicopters flew up and around, contorting themselves into various flight patterns. A Harrier jump jet hovered for ages over the water alongside before embarking on a round of crowd-pleasing manoeuvres. All the while, naval ratings were passing through the throng with magnums of champagne, dispensing from them as if they were about to go out of fashion. This was clearly going to be no ordinary award luncheon, this was a Scottish piss up par excellence, the like of which the English could never hope to equal.

Sometime after one o'clock, the assembled group was encouraged to descend to the adjacent marquee, which had been set up on the quayside. Where earlier the guests had moved sprightly up the gangplank, they now decanted themselves slowly and purposefully down onto the dockside. We found our table, which, like all the others, was heaving with bottles of alcohol – not just wine but liqueurs and port as well. The menu was excellent although what we ate I cannot accurately remember. Speeches followed, one Scotsman after another lauding the auld country and its business excellence. The Lord Chancellor, Lord Mackay of Clashfern, guest of honour, spoke, as did the recipient of the award, Sir Tom Farmer, the Quick Fit fitter, but this lunch was certainly no quick fit.

At around four o'clock, Cameron decided we should think about leaving and sent one of his minions, who had been sitting with us, to find a taxi. Not too many of the guests had the stamina to tackle the largish miniatures of port and brandy laid out by each place. 'Is this good port?' Cameron asked his neighbour. 'Aye, Cameron, it's vintage,' was the reply, which encouraged Cameron to load his pockets with bottles left unopened by the departing guests. We got up to leave, Cameron's bottles clanking as we moved off.

Outside, we found his functionary weaving round in circles, seemingly oblivious of what else was going on. 'Och, we'll no be waiting for him,' said Cameron as we moved towards the road. Fortunately, we found a taxi straight away and I was able to drop off Cameron in the centre of Edinburgh before going on to the airport. I marvelled on the flight home at the way in which the Scots entertained themselves all the while wondering whether that poor man was still wandering round in circles by the dockside.

During Patrick Deuchar's tenure, my work at the Royal Albert Hall increased each year; especially so in 1993 when the hall decided that all the disparate Christmas concerts should be put together under one banner. Patrick invited me to take over the pre-Christmas slot and so I found myself trying to placate a number of organisations that had traditionally been presenting their own individual Christmas events there and who now felt they were being kicked out. I managed to keep a number of these events within the Christmas Festival framework that I developed. The hall's management was looking for more intensive use of the available dates and a better financial return, both of which I was able to achieve for them. By 2002, the Christmas Festival was playing to ninety-four per cent capacity overall, a percentage which was maintained throughout my stewardship.

During his time at the hall, Patrick married for the third time. Liz Robertson was the widow and eighth wife of Alan J. Lerner, the lyricist and writer who, together with composer Frederick Loewe, created *My Fair Lady* and a number of other Broadway musicals. The wedding took place at St Paul's Covent Garden with the reception held at the nearby Theatre Museum. I was surprised to see nobody present from the Royal Albert Hall but the hall itself was still well represented, with house champagne, liveried catering staff and assorted canapés familiar to any regulars at the hall.

In the years leading up to the Millennium, there had been a lot of speculation in the press that somebody had booked the date at the Royal Albert Hall twenty-five years previously. The hall kept very quiet about their plans, although I do know that Harvey Goldsmith at one time had an elaborate scheme for a gala evening involving linking the hall to the Royal Geographical Society nearby with a temporary walkway. In the event, I was surprised and elated when the hall's then CEO David Elliott asked me – for whatever reason – around April 1999 whether I could put together something appropriate for New Year's Eve and New Year's Day. I never did discover how far down the line they had got with whatever it was they had been planning for so many years but it did not really matter. Even if the invitation just eight months prior to the night itself meant that I was 'the lender of last resort', I could still enjoy the moment which everyone was so keenly anticipating.

I first of all approached John Manger, who was then CEO of the Royal Philharmonic. For three concerts, one on New Year's Eve and two on New Year's Day, he quoted me a fee roughly three times the normal rate. Using General McAuliffe's famous one-word response when the American 101st Airborne Division found itself encircled at Bastogne in the Battle of the Bulge and was asked by the Germans to surrender, I replied, 'Nuts!' It seemed to me the only rational response I could make to such an outrageous and economically suicidal offer. My friend Ian Maclay was then running the BBC Concert Orchestra and provided a much more reasonable quote which I was happy to accept.

I booked singers and a pianist for 'Rhapsody in Blue', plus two dancers from the English National Ballet to perform the *Swan Lake* pas de deux. Tamara Rojo, then still with ENB before her move to the Royal Ballet, was going to perform but her partner was indisposed and so, at short notice, she asked Yat-Sen Chang to dance with her. We had to change from *Swan Lake* to *Don Quixote* but it did not matter in the least. The two of them gave a stunning performance of the famous pas de deux from Minkus's ballet, fiery and spectacular. Christopher Warren Greene conducted the three performances which were packed out. It was a great start to the New Year and the new Millennium. And, needless to say, the cash machines which were all predicted to fail at midnight because of the Millennium bug, continued as normal.

CHAPTER TWENTY

OPERA GOES COMMERCIAL

The experiences with *Turandot* and the Royal Opera House at Wembley had taught me a great deal. Clearly Wembley was too remote a location for these types of productions. Whereas pop fans were willing to travel anywhere to see the acts, the opera audience was much more likely to support a venue more centrally located. So I pondered for quite a while on whether the Royal Albert Hall could work for 'opera in the round', with the audience seated around three-hundred-and-sixty degrees. Placing the action in the middle is challenging for the director but allows for great spectacle coupled with a real feeling of a shared experience, with the audience packed all round and concentrating together on the action in the centre.

Meanwhile, as *Classical Spectacular* continued to do so well, in 1995 the hall suggested trying out an opera version 'in the round' with excerpts from a number of different operas. I had seen George Benson performing in the hall on a revolving stage in the middle of the arena and this convinced me that moving the action to the centre of the hall with the audience all around the performers would work well.

I engaged Michael Hunt to stage the programme and he did a first-class job in putting together excerpts including scenes from *La Bohème* and *Carmen*, *The Pearfishers* duet (of course) and the last act of *Tosca*, though in this instance the soprano Susan Bullock had to stab herself as of course there was nowhere appropriate for her to fling herself from. The hall was impressed with the results and I wondered if it was not now time for us to enter the arena opera market once more.

It so happened that the following year, 1996, was the centenary of *La Bohème* and neither the ROH nor ENO was planning to do performances. So

I suggested to Patrick Deuchar that we should together stage an in-the-round production at the hall in February when there was a clear run of dates available. I thought our strategy should be to plan to do up to ten performances but only initially announce five so that if bookings were not good we were only committed to the smaller number. Patrick agreed.

Michael Hunt was re-engaged to direct *La Bohème* and James Lockhart came in as musical director. I had first worked with James years earlier in the opera concert I had presented in Cardiff when he had persuaded Margaret Price to take part. He was an established and reliable opera conductor with a great deal of practical experience. We decided on double casts and assembled a really good group of soloists. William Dazeley and Christopher Maltman would share Marcello; Susan Bullock as one of the Mimis and Vivian Tierney as Musetta. The problem was that Michael got carried away and decided he wanted 'international' singers for the first cast. Foolishly, or perhaps naively, we let him go ahead and though the soprano and tenor he persuaded us to book were both adequate, they hardly justified the cost and effort involved. I never understood why on earth when we had Susan Bullock she was not given the first performance.

Turandot at Wembley had given me a practical insight into staging opera on a large scale. However, at the Royal Albert Hall we had to start from scratch. Heather Walker, the hall's deputy director, proved a tower of strength in terms of sorting out the complicated issues involved with regards to the hall itself. Having made the decision to stage the production in the round, we had to work with a revised seat manifest (effectively the seating plan) which cut the seating capacity because the arena seating would become the stage. This is an extremely complicated issue at the Royal Albert Hall because of the debenture seats which are owned by the members.

Before the Royal Albert Hall opened in 1871, the committee charged with building it realised there was not enough money to complete the building work. So they asked for subscribers to give money and in return they were offered a 999-year lease on one or more seats, depending on the amount each had subscribed. In the end, they sold around fourteen hundred seats, all of course in prime positions, including all but three of the Grand Tier boxes, the majority of the Loggia boxes and a number of the smaller Second Tier boxes plus around seven hundred stalls seats. For performances designated as 'ordinary lettings' the members have the right to use their seats or to resell them as they wish, not necessarily via the hall's box office. This accounts for why tickets sometimes come onto the secondary market via ticket agencies at seemingly very high prices for popular events. For those events designated as 'exclusive lettings', the members have no special rights and all the tickets are put on general sale. The whole procedure is governed by Act of Parliament and the members' seats themselves are known to change hands at very high prices, a Grand Tier box having once reportedly been sold for over £2 million. As *La Bohème* was a staged production (rather than a concert), different rules applied, which meant that many more 'exclusive' lettings could be made available. As the hall was coming in as a co-promoter, sharing the risk with us, there was an incentive for them to maximise the box office income.

Booking the orchestra was easy – Ian Maclay was still running the BBC Concert Orchestra so we booked them. The chorus was more difficult but with the right contacts we were able to book many of the chorus members who sang at Glyndebourne during the summer season there. The stage management and technical crew somehow emerged almost as a group from amongst the many seasoned professionals working in this area. Andrew Bridge, who did the lighting for our production of *La Bohème* and would go on to work on all the operas at the ROH over the following years, was an absolute miracle worker who could light a show while rehearsals and walk-throughs were going on, continuing on through the night to get it all done. The time we had in the hall to fit up and dress-rehearse was very limited.

Bookings opened well and it was clear from the start that we would easily fill five shows and probably some of the others as well. Peter Thompson, the wonderful PR guru, organised a lunch for the major arts correspondent from the National Press for Patrick Deuchar and me to announce our plans. Patrick was seated at one end of the table and I at the other. In response to various questions, I started to give some of-the-cuff comments about our experiences with the Royal Opera House at Wembley and what I saw were some of the problems over at Covent Garden. The reporters started taking notes and more questions followed. Patrick looked decidedly embarrassed and left early. Alone with the journalists, I continued for another half hour or so.

Although I had not exactly planned it this way, I knew well enough that we would get precious little coverage without adding something controversial. So I tossed in a few well-chosen comments about the exclusivity engendered by the Royal Opera House and the accompanying snobbishness. I was right; the next day most of the papers gave coverage to my comments and very quickly radio and television joined in. Jeremy Isaacs, still director of the ROH, was beside himself trying to defend his position and I suddenly found myself live on air on the BBC debating with Nicholas Payne, still then at the ROH but later to move onto ENO, who had been pulled out of a rehearsal and into the BBC radio car. The controversy continued and I realised that it was likely to prove a high-risk strategy on my part as I felt that I was probably setting myself up for a fall once the production was reviewed. However, most of what I was saying about the ROH struck home.

Bohème rehearsals started in Toynbee Hall, where John Profumo worked out his penance after the Christine Keeler affair. Then, once the chorus joined, we moved to Three Mills Island near Bow. Michael Hunt, who had been so good with the *Opera Spectacular*, was now clearly under much more pressure. It did not make for an ideal atmosphere but the production was coming together rather well. The final rehearsals moved to the hall and we prepared for the first night.

The audience loved it; the critics hated it and I was savaged by a number of the press for daring to present commercial opera in London. Nonetheless, the word of mouth was good, we added all five extra performances and the production handsomely paid its way. It was not perfect, far from it. It looked good, the set designs worked well and the costumes by John Bright, who had won an Oscar for his designs for the 1985 film *A Room with a View*, were delightfully authentic. But the sound certainly was not as good as it might have been. The purists were horrified by the idea of amplified opera but I never understood how you could stage these types of productions without sound enhancement. In-the-round staging means that artists will not always be facing the entire audience and cannot produce acoustically the necessary level of sound throughout the auditorium. Moreover, it has to be admitted that audiences used to listening to music through personal headphones or even on modern digital radios are more attuned to a certain clarity of sound which, without any enhancement, would be missing.

It had been an ordeal by fire but we had come through it and now both the hall and I wanted to make plans for the following year. We agreed on *Carmen* and Patrick was keen for us to approach Frank Dunlop. Frank turned out to be utterly charming. I knew of him as a distinguished director at the National Theatre, founder of the Young Vic and more recently as the Director of the Edinburgh Festival. Though I started to get worried when he suggested we move the production to one end of the hall, rather destroying the idea of opera in the round. However, Patrick liked the idea and it was settled on. Frank had no definite thoughts about a designer and gave us a list to work through as to who might be available. Ralph Koltai was and came up with an impressive design, which would have seemed quite revolutionary thirty years earlier.

Rehearsals started and, as was my wont, I kept an eye on them, dropping in every few days to see how they were getting along. I could sense the atmosphere was not good. Frank did not seem to be doing very much directing from his chair at one end of the room. When the quintet in Act II was rehearsed for the first time, the cast members involved looked to Frank for guidance. 'Let's see how it runs,' he said, leaving them to their own devices. They told me later that he never gave them any further notes on it. It stayed much as they had let it happen at the first rehearsal. It was not a good sign.

The press was once again unenthusiastic and this time I felt the public reaction was not as good as for *La Bohème*, although business over the twelve shows was decent. I cannot say it was a particularly bad production. It was nicely sung, it looked pretty and the big numbers were as stirring as ever. It is just that we had missed a trick. *Carmen* is the ideal opera for staging in the round in the Royal Albert Hall where the shape of the bullring already exists and yet we had allowed Frank to take the easy option and move the production to almost end-on. I felt sorry for Frank as whatever was heaped on me in the press was even more so heaped on him and he had just had a similar experience a few days earlier with *Heathcliff*, a musical adapted from *Wuthering Heights*, in which he had directed Cliff Richard and had opened to appalling notices, much of them directed against Frank.

.....

Patrick did not appear to notice; he seemed in thrall to Frank, even going so far as to praise individual scenes that he thought had been beautifully directed. I wondered if we could continue. *La Bohème* and *Carmen* had both been profitable but they were not moving the cause of arena opera forward to any degree.

The one really positive thing to come out of *Carmen* was the sound designed by Bobbie Aitken. He managed to greatly improve what we had achieved with *La Bohème* and over the years the system he uses has moved forward in leaps and bounds, providing pinpoint accurate delivery to every part of the house. This has meant that when any of the soloists move the sound follows them, so that audience members facing them will be aware of sound coming directly from their mouths whereas those now behind will hear the sound as though the singers have their backs to them. As the singers are forever moving around, this provides the sound designer with an incredibly complicated scenario which has to be plotted to the nth degree.

We decided to do *Madam Butterfly* next. Patrick and I had been expecting to talk with David Freeman as a possible director but he had not shown up on the appointed day of our meeting. We started negotiations with another director but then these became bogged down over what we thought were unreasonable requests from his agent. But just as these negotiations came to a halt, Patrick had a call from David asking to reschedule his visit as he'd had to rush to the dentist at the time of the earlier appointment. I think we were both a bit half-hearted about seeing him but we fixed a meeting. If ever there was a defining moment in the history of in-the-round opera at the Royal Albert Hall it was this meeting.

From the word go, I found myself totally convinced by David's thoughts and ideas. Here was somebody I could do business with and it was quite unexpected as he had a reputation whilst running Opera Factory of doing very outré and avant-garde work and I had not thought that he was the sort of director who would be interested in working in a commercial environment. But it seemed I had misjudged both the challenge and the attraction of working on a production at the Royal Albert Hall. As here was David proposing ideas and making suggestions that seemed absolutely right for our situation. He instinctively understood what we were trying to achieve and we felt he would be absolutely the right man for the job. We more or less hired him on the spot.

Together with David Roger, his designer, he came up with a tremendous idea for staging the opera which would allow the intimate scenes to be tightly focused while maintaining the spectacle. They wanted to create a Japanese water garden and flood the arena of the hall with sixty-five thousand litres of water. My ideas for marketing and publicity immediately went into overdrive. I could see wonderful opportunities with the stories about flooding the hall right in the forefront.

David took an immediate and close interest in every detail of the production. He asked us to commission Amanda Holden to make a new translation and he suggested Peter Robinson to us as musical director. Both he and Peter attended every audition as we searched for the elusive Asian sopranos to play the title role. At one of the auditions, a young Chinese singer who had been living in Canada came to sing for us. It may sound like an old show-business cliché but we knew instinctively that we had found one of the two artists we needed to play Butterfly. Liping Zhang was quite sensational and we were very fortunate to get Nancy Yuen as the other Butterfly.

David's style in rehearsal was quite different from anything we had seen before. He took time to talk over his ideas with the cast and to explain how he saw the production evolving. He spent even more time with individuals and groups of artists going through how they would tackle each scene. There were never any tantrums, just clear-headed, calm directions. Everyone felt comfortable and the stage management team, always the first to sense these things, felt we were on to a winner.

The first night was incredible. I hid in my box not out of nerves but simply to avoid having to talk to any of the many people I knew would be there, at least until after it was over. The reaction was astounding – at the conclusion of the final chord the applause started and continued for several minutes. Deborah Warner, Elaine Paige and Peter Hall all came up to offer congratulations along with a host of friends and colleagues. It was a great moment and I felt we had finally cracked it. The next morning, *The Times* ran a headline 'Gubbay Strikes Gold with Arena Butterfly'. It was to be the first of many such rave reviews. The few tickets that were still unsold were quickly taken and we had to squeeze in an extra two shows, which was all that the very tight schedule would allow. Had we been able, such was the demand for seats that we could probably have continued for another two or even three weeks.

Patrick Deuchar, meanwhile, had left the hall and was not even present for the first night of *Butterfly*. I never knew the reason but I was sorry to see him go. In many ways he did a fantastic job at the hall. He instigated a bid for lottery money and oversaw the application, which resulted in the hall being awarded £40 million. He also managed to keep the hall open virtually throughout the period of the rebuilding work. It was a remarkable achievement and it is all the more sad that he did not stay on to see it through. David Elliott, who had been Patrick's deputy, was appointed as the new chief executive, a very popular choice with both staff and promoters.

With David Freeman and David Rogers, I now felt that we had in place the perfect team for staging popular and exciting arena opera at the Royal Albert Hall. The next year, they worked together on Tosca and there was never any doubt about what we should do the following year. *Madam Butterfly* was once again a huge success and has since been revived again – not I think, for the last time. Liping Zhang and Nancy Yuen returned to share performances of the title role with Keith Latham back as Sharpless. In many ways, Keith had, to my mind, been the most outstanding of all in the original run. He had made the character of the American consul, so often played as a two-dimensional, cut-out character, into somebody real. He was greatly moved by Liping's portrayal of the title role and cried genuine tears in the dress rehearsal during their scene together in the second act. He was also wonderful as *Tosca*'s Scarpia and was becoming a more or less permanent member of our annual Albert Hall casts.

After the revival of *Madam Butterfly*, we decided with the hall to mount a production of *Aida* to mark the Verdi centenary. Keith was due to sing some performances as Amonasro, the Ethiopian king and Aida's father. Soon after the start of rehearsals, he went to Birmingham to sing in my Verdi Centenary Gala, which was going to be repeated the following day at the Barbican. I was on the train to Paris with my younger daughter and my grandson, Ben, when my mobile rang. It was a colleague with the deeply distressing news that Keith had been found dead in his dressing room at Symphony Hall where he had gone to rest after the rehearsal. He had suffered a massive heart attack. As he was not required right at the start of the concert, his absence was not noticed until a little later. Robin Stapleton, the conductor, and the other soloists had somehow managed to get through the programme having to adapt and change items more or less on the hoof. They did not know that Keith had died until the end of the performance.

The next day, I returned to London from Paris and joined the artists and the conductor on stage at the start of the Barbican concert. It was a difficult moment as I had to explain to the audience that Keith was not going to appear. We dedicated both the concert and the production of *Aida* to his memory. A few days later, I attended his funeral in Burnley where he had been a leading light with local music societies before deciding in his late twenties to study professionally. At forty-six, he had been at the height of his powers with a great future ahead of him; now his career had been cruelly cut short. Whenever I think of *Madam Butterfly* I recall Keith, a great performer and a wonderful team player. I miss him still.

The opera in the round productions continued annually. Then in 2001, Nicholas Payne from ENO got in touch with David Elliott at the hall about a possible production which David suggested should involve me too. ENO wanted to bring *The Magic Flute* to RAH in a new production by Deborah Warner, which was a really exciting proposition. We had a preliminary meeting at the hall when Nick outlined Deborah's proposals, which included, if I recall this correctly, an element of live animals including a panther. The initial excitement was beginning to be tempered by some concern when the news came through that Nick Payne was leaving ENO and the project was shelved.

However, the hall had pencilled dates in October 2002 for the production and I floated the idea of mounting another opera production instead. The hall was unwilling to go ahead on the usual co-promotion basis so I ended up rather foolishly undertaking the whole thing myself. The Intermezzo from *Cavalleria Rusticana* was always among the ten most popular pieces on Classic FM so I took the plunge and scheduled the opera alongside its eternal twin, *I Pagliacci*. We booked a tremendous cast, Martin Duncan put together a wonder pair of productions and Alison Chitty produced fabulous designs. The critics were generally enthusiastic but the public didn't come in sufficient numbers and I ended up facing a loss of half a million pounds. It once again demonstrated the fine line I had to tread to find opera and ballet that worked commercially. For whatever reason, *Cav* and *Pag* were outside this narrow band.

Had ENO gone ahead with Deborah Warner's *Magic Flute*, that would have been something special. How it would have sold I am not sure but it would have given ENO a chance to try something on an altogether different scale with a great director away from the Coliseum. When ENO moved to the Coliseum in 1968, there had been so much goodwill for it to succeed. It had a wonderful permanent band of singers and could cast a great deal of the repertoire from the core company. The powerhouse years under David Pountney, Mark Elder and Peter Jonas ended however in 1992 and since then ENO has found it more and more difficult to sustain a permanent company providing a full season of opera. It is now down to a rump of a season of eighty-plus performances squeezed into a short season so that the rest of the time the Coliseum can be rented out to commercial West End producers. Lilian Baylis who founded Sadler's Wells Opera (ENO's precursor) would not have been happy to see the sad decline of a once great national company.

Back at the hall in 2002, in what had now become the traditional February spot, David Freeman mounted *Carmen* with a design by David Rodgers. It provided colour and spectacle and has been revived several times. It made me realise how tame our production a few years earlier had been. This new production looked good and had a rousing final act with fire eaters and acrobats as well as toreadors, picadors and the mayor and townsfolk.

As originally conceived by Bizet, *Carmen*, which was written for the Opera Comique in Paris, had spoken dialogue between the musical numbers. The recitatives (sung dialogue) so beloved of major opera houses were added later and do not work nearly so well as dialogue. David had provided his own translation of the dialogue, although he had opened this out rather too liberally and it took some effort to get him to reduce it in length.

Carmen is undoubtedly the biggest crowd pleaser amongst the handful of operas that can be produced on an arena scale. Though it always

......

surprised me how *Madam Butterfly* also proved so successful with audiences at the Royal Albert Hall. This venue is unique as it provides an auditorium with five thousand seats but still has an intimacy which allows the audience for both opera and ballet to be drawn close to the action. The sense of shared experience created by five thousand people encircling the arena stage, whether concentrating on an intimate scene or looking out onto a colourful crowd scene with the action going on all around, is powerful indeed.

Francesca Zambello's production of *La Bohème*, first staged in 2006, was always a favourite of mine. The scene in the Café Momus which exploded at the end of Act I was incredible. She managed to create little vignettes of people in post-war Paris, each character an individual with an easily readable backstory. Francesca was the most lovely person to work with, the company adored her and she made a point of learning everyone's name at an early stage of rehearsals.

The in-the-round operas continued annually for almost twenty years and were for me the high spot of the year. There was incredible enthusiasm amongst the regular team of chorus, orchestra and stage management; a real sense of camaraderie and great pride in what we were able to achieve together.

CHAPTER TWENTY-ONE

JOB APPLICATION

My first visit to the Royal Opera House was sometime in the mid-1950s when my brother and I were taken by our parents to see *Carmen*. I can still remember the feeling of excitement at being in such a marvellous theatre and being impressed by the spectacle onstage. Though this was marred a little, even in my child's mind, when the chorus ladies, standing on balconies, started fanning themselves like good Spanish senoritas. Their movement caused the balconies and their supporting 'flats', or scenery, around them to sway slightly, briefly breaking the illusion of a perfect setting.

My dad would often take my mum to see performances at the ROH. He even had the chance to meet the great Italian tenor Beniamino Gigli when he was asked to advise him on his tax affairs concerning his appearance at the ROH soon after the war. Dad recalled meeting him in his suite at the Savoy Hotel where he was staying, surrounded by a retinue of assistants, managers and advisers. The hotel manager was translating for him and every time my dad spelt out the – very limited – options available, Gigli, outraged at the amount of tax that he had to pay on his fees, would rise to his feet saying, '*Non e giusto!*' (it isn't fair) at which point his entire retinue would rise with him as one, repeating in chorus, '*Non e giusto!*'

This must have been shortly after the opera company was formed from scratch. Unlike the pre-war opera seasons, this was now a permanent company with its own orchestra (shared with the Royal Ballet), chorus and principal singers. Indeed, for many years, the opera performed with casts largely drawn from the resident roster of singers, and very good they were too. At the same time, international guest artists were employed and there was a happy match between the two. The members of the resident company enjoyed security and could take on roles outside of the ROH as well.

The original general manager, Sir David Webster, who, before the war, was chief executive of a department store in Liverpool, was a rather stiff and unbending character but he ran a tight ship with limited public subsidy and virtually no sponsorship, which barely existed at the time. His successor, John Tooley (later Sir John), who had been his deputy for many years, carried on under much the same conditions and continued to see the Royal Opera prosper. Jeremy Isaacs was appointed in 1987 to succeed Tooley, after Isaacs had failed to get the top job at the BBC. He had enjoyed a successful career in television, including producing the landmark series *The World at War*, and had been the founding chief executive at Channel 4. Perhaps knowing that the job of chief executive of the Royal Opera House was his second choice was not a great way to start his time there.

There was concern about the way that opera stars could literally 'call the tune', leading to higher prices and elitism on a grand scale. How could it be right to pay vast fees to Pavarotti to appear in only three or four performances where the tickets were almost solely available for the regular, well-endowed patrons of the ROH? How could millions of pounds of public subsidy be justified when the only beneficiaries were a small clique of opera lovers who, in any case, could afford to pay even more for the tickets? In these circumstances, why subsidise the Royal Opera at all when, at that time, whole parts of the country lacked easy access to symphony concerts, opera and full-scale ballet? Why not use the public subsidy where it could have much greater benefit?

In my own work, I have ventured treading the delicate line between what has to be subsidised and what can be mounted commercially but I have always supported the notion of public subsidy for the arts all my working life. I have gone on record in countless interviews over the years making the point that without public subsidy we would not have great opera, theatre and ballet companies, world-class orchestras and great museums and galleries. At this time, however, I did question why the ROH enjoyed such a privileged position from the public purse.

Jeremy Isaacs was happy to allow television cameras in for a fly-on-the-wall documentary, *The House*, which aired in 1996. Considering that his background prior to his appointment at the ROH was in television, it seems hard to understand why he could have encouraged the programme, opening up as it did the Opera House to intense public scrutiny over which he had no control. It was good for the wider public to see how its taxes were being spent and it was very entertaining for the millions who tuned in each week to watch it, but it was hardly a public relations success and Isaacs never appeared to be terribly comfortable throughout the series. His remarks to an incredulous taxi driver about how he could get change out of one hundred pounds if he took his wife to Covent Garden, of course with the caveat that he would have to sit high up in the house, sticks firmly in my mind.

Covent Garden, at least the opera side, was seen at the time as an inefficient and patrician-like organisation pandering largely to the needs of a small group of opera goers. The decision by Lord Gowrie, as chairman of the Arts Council, to immediately dole out tens of millions of National Lottery funds to Covent Garden for its redevelopment was badly handled. It was in the very early stages of the lottery and, with the ROH as the cheerleader, it seemed intent on funding, at least initially, an elitist and narrow range of projects geared towards London and the south east. The news coverage showing some of those involved swigging champagne in celebration merely underlined the message. Jeremy Isaacs, now beknighted, left the ROH later in 1996.

It had been long envisaged that the Opera House would need to close for some time to allow for expansion and improvement of its facilities, though work was repeatedly delayed and no alternative venue was secured. In the event, even though the Royal Opera could have moved lock, stock and barrel to the Lyceum Theatre down the road, indecision meant it was left with a season at Sadler's Wells and peripatetic forays to the Shaftesbury Theatre and the Barbican Theatre. Meanwhile, the company's finances were in a state of near bankruptcy. Isaacs's successor, Genista McIntosh, lasted under five months before she resigned through ill health. It seemed to me at the time that her position was undermined by the elements on the Opera House board who were not comfortable with her ideas of democratising the ROH.

There followed a move worthy of Pooh-Bah, the Lord High Everything Else, himself. Mary Allen, who was secretary-general of the Arts Council, and who had sat in on the interviewing board that had appointed Genista McIntosh, was put forward to take on the now-vacant ROH position by Lord

Chadlington, chairman of the board of the ROH, without the appointment being advertised. Chris Smith, newly appointed culture secretary, was reluctantly persuaded to endorse this even though it apparently breached the Arts Council's own funding conditions. The former hoofer from Godspell and The Rocky Horror Show now found herself with a greatly enhanced salary, in charge of Covent Garden.

According to her diaries, later published in *The Times*, she suddenly found out the truth about the ROH's deep financial mess. All the time she had been at the Arts Council, she was apparently unaware that her principal client, the organisation which year after year took the largest single grant, was in a huge hole, apparently at one point just minutes away from going under. Later the same year, a House of Commons Select Committee under Gerald Kauffman MP, was highly critical of Allen. The board of the ROH resigned en masse but Mary Allen managed to hang on for a further four months. She left after the arrival of Colin Southgate, the new chairman of the board; whether it is true that a substantial redundancy payoff was made is unclear. One estimate of the cost that year of paying off three chief executives plus sundry other senior figures was over £1.5 million.

Mary Allen's brief appointment was followed by an interregnum. Pelham Allen (no relation) was a consultant with Coopers and Lybrand who were paid a substantial sum out of public funds to leave their man in place while the ROH searched for yet another chief executive. Michael Kaiser had been running the American Ballet Theater and was credited with having turned around its fortunes. Now he was recruited to run Covent Garden and would oversee the opening of the house after the refurbishment had been completed. At least he brought some stability and calm to what had become a fractious and divided house.

When Covent Garden was putting together its plans for the official reopening of the refurbished ROH, I found out that my name was apparently scratched off the guest list. I took this as a compliment; it meant that at least my occasional comments about them had been striking home.

Michael Kaiser remained for less than one year after the reopening amidst stories that he was unhappy living in London. During this time, the ROH managed a beautiful own goal when they suddenly cancelled a special schools' matinee of Harrison Birtwistle's Gawain. A large number of disappointed schoolchildren had been preparing for their visit to Covent Garden. I was able to invite many of them to see Madame Butterfly at the Royal Albert Hall.

That, then, was the background leading up to my decision, when it was announced that Kaiser was leaving, to throw my hat into the ring. I had no particular intention of giving up the day job, it was simply an opportunity to make a little mischief and gain publicity for my forthcoming opera production at the Royal Albert Hall – it was too good an opportunity to miss. So in September 2000, I wrote to Heather Newill, who was handling the recruitment of the new chief executive on behalf of the ROH. I made it clear that I was making a 'corporate application' on behalf of my company. Somehow, with a little appropriate help, the press got to hear of this and a huge amount of publicity was generated in the media.

One of the first questions put to me was how I intended to get along with the chairman, Sir Colin Southgate, as I had been rather rude about him in the past. I responded robustly by saying that he would certainly have to go were I to get the job. After all, anyone who had said (as Southgate famously had done) that they did not want to sit next to somebody wearing shorts and smelly trainers at Covent Garden was hardly likely to endear themselves to a more democratically run opera house. I also prepared a twelve-point plan for dealing with the ROH. The 'job application' may have been rather tongue-in-cheek but I was in earnest when I wrote this plan. It involved better use of resources at Covent Garden including separating the opera and ballet seasons to enable a more intensive schedule of performances.

I was surprised by the amount of interest and support I received. The *Observer*, *Guardian* and *Sunday Times* all ran interviews and profiles, while *The Times* had two separate pieces both supporting the application. In the end, the ROH refused to accept the application, which was entirely predictable, and would not grant me, or rather 'us', an interview, as this was a corporate application. I think that was another miscalculation on their part – they would have received a better press if they had been seen to go through the interview process. Had they entered more fully into the debate, instead of almost pretending that the application was not happening, they might at least have been able to score some points in their favour. My twelve-point memorandum had struck home and was favourably commented upon but they could have put up a tenable counter argument.

In the end, the ROH appointed Tony Hall from BBC News as their chief executive. Tony Hall is urbane and charming and at last somebody who knew how to handle the media headed the ROH. His tenure there, before returning to the BBC as Director General, brought back stability and pride to a great national institution. The appointment of Ross Stretton to head the Royal Ballet was somewhat disastrous, however, with the board of the Royal Opera House clearly having failed in their duty to adequately check his background, leading to him leaving within a year of his appointment. Covent Garden, true as ever to the weak organisation that it was, paid him off his full contract. Yet more taxpayers' money was being thrown away.

A few months after my corporate application was rejected by the Opera House, I was awarded the CBE. Quite why or how this came about I could not work out as I had never ever thought about this and I originally considered the letter from the prime minister's office was a joke. I later reflected that maybe, just maybe, somebody in the Establishment quite liked my taking on Covent Garden and calling it to account.

CHAPTER TWENTY-TWO

DISASTERS AND MISHAPS

I am very often asked about the worst disaster I have faced and people invariably want to know about things going wrong during performances. There have been plenty of those and I will get cracking on them later but first I must recall the Savoy Opera project. It had nothing to do with Gilbert and Sullivan's Savoy Operas but rather a project to present opera in the West End which went disastrously wrong. The hardest thing for an impresario to say to an interesting opportunity is 'no', as I learnt once more to my cost.

Sir Stephen Waley-Cohen ran the Savoy Theatre and harboured a real desire to present opera there. With thirteen hundred seats, it was an ideal size and it also had the inestimable advantage of having retained its orchestra pit, whereas most West End theatres had long ago dispensed with theirs in order to add more seats. My original discussions with Stephen in 2004 centred on programming a six-week season of one opera, followed by the next and so on. Stephen had a group of outside investors willing to put up money for the initial season of six or eight works and Stephen and I also made an investment. We appointed an artistic team to run the project. They auditioned hundreds of singers but the casting in the end was not as good as I believe we would have achieved using our in-house resources. The team also decided to run two operas together in one tranche, which made it more difficult to market and advertise as we were obliged to push each pair of operas rather than concentrating on a single title.

Bookings were slow in spite of an enormous amount of press interest. The opening two productions drew a wide range of notices, some of which were actually rather good. But the lighting for both productions was underwhelming; the sets were uninspired even though the costumes were great. Two of the three making up the artistic team never attended a performance.

The box office remained stagnant and we made the difficult decision to cut our losses after the initial two productions had finished their runs. The press had a field day; I went to Paris on a Friday and turned off my phone. When I returned on Monday and reconnected my phone, there were over one hundred missed calls, virtually all from the journalists. The furore soon died down and the old adage of 'today's newspapers are tomorrow's chip papers' proved yet again to be correct.

Other disasters were more about individual performances. *Carmen* at the O2 was a case in point, though it wasn't so much a disaster as a walk on the wild side. In 2010, for whatever reason, the usual opera slot at the Royal Albert Hall in February was not available. Meanwhile, the O2 had been pressing me to do more there beyond the initial Christmas concert I had tried with them. So I thought it would be interesting to take David Freeman's production of *Carmen*, which I really liked and which we had done a couple of times at the RAH, to the O2. We scheduled three performances over a Saturday and Sunday. Then came the rub.

The O2, which was co-promoting the dates with me, rather fancied putting the winner of *Popstar to Operastar*, some television reality show, into the production as Escamillo, the toreador. I thought it was a dubious gimmick but was eventually pressured into agreeing for him to do one performance. It certainly wasn't dreadful, indeed it wasn't even bad; it was actually quite respectable. Ah, but the cost – not in financial terms, but in stress and worry for the poor music staff. Eventually, our wonderful assistant conductor was made up as one of the chorus gentlemen and went onstage to act as prompter almost underneath Escamillo's nose. In the end I breathed a sigh of relief; it had gone all right.

The O2 was also the venue of another interesting performance. They had booked *An Evening with Julie Andrews* and already had another promoter onboard with them but wanted me along as well. All the promotional material made it very clear that she wasn't singing other than a couple of numbers. A botched operation some years earlier had damaged her vocal cords and it was well known that she could no longer perform as she once had. In fact, she was going to narrate *Simian's Gift*, a piece written by her daughter, in which she would be accompanied not only by an orchestra but also by some outstanding Broadway performers. Elizabeth Taylor, by then confined to a wheelchair, came backstage in the interval and there were many well-known faces in the audience.

Alas, 'the best laid plans of mice and men', as Robert Burns put it, go awry. Some people were clearly expecting to hear her sing more and there were a number who left before the end. Someone from BBC's *Watchdog* programme left a message for me to call as they wanted me to appear on the programme. I rang back the researcher and said I would be happy to answer any and all of her questions but I would not appear on *Watchdog*. She was pleasantly surprised by my candour and I made no attempt to duck any of the questions she put to me. I said that I was of course disappointed to learn that some people were unhappy but we had advertised the programme details correctly and Dame Julie herself in pre-show interviews had been at pains to point out that she would be doing very little singing. I was glad to be associated with promoting the show but of course disappointed that not everyone was happy. Julie Andrews was an absolute joy to work with, utterly charming and very easy to get on with. It had been quite an evening but I wouldn't have wanted to miss it, not for the world.

Disasters onstage are fortunately a rarity. Though when we brought *Carmen* back to the RAH after its journey out to south-east London at the O2, I found myself having to go onstage to explain to the audience that our Don Jose had lost his voice after the 'Flower Song' and that one of the smugglers would sing the part from where the orchestra were playing whilst the voiceless Jose would mime his way through the rest of the opera. The new voice of Jose was magnificent and received thunderous applause at the end, as did the chorus member who had stepped into his role as one of the smugglers. Such incidents are rare but when they happen it always amazes me how the artists pull together and carry on by hook or by crook. The camaraderie is intense; the show must go on.

On another occasion, dear Heather Walker, the RAH's deputy director, had to ask the audience at a performance of *Classical Spectacular* to cross their legs as the water level in the loos had dropped alarmingly owing to a nearby leak.

CHAPTER TWENTY-THREE

BALLET

The staging of arena opera at the Royal Albert Hall led directly to an approach from English National Ballet. Carole McPhee, their general administrator, had been to see *La Bohème* and had subsequently brought Derek Deane, the artistic director, across from their offices a couple of hundred yards from the hall to see the set-up. Now they proposed developing arena ballet, starting with *Swan Lake*. The hall was enthusiastic and gave the go-ahead for the following summer, June 1997. Derek Deane's ideas for transforming *Swan Lake* from its traditional end-on format to a full in-the-round version were developed using small coins to represent the dancers placed on an enlarged ground plan of the hall's arena.

With sixty-five swans and a total company of one hundred and twenty dancers, there was a genuinely spectacular feel to the production. I went to a couple of early rehearsals at ENB's own studios before they moved to much larger premises for the final weeks of rehearsals with the full company. Now the project could be seen transformed into the giant production it had become with Derek and his assistants marshalling the dancers into the kaleidoscope of shapes which were to be its hallmark.

The first performance of *Swan Lake* was very well received with the two guest artists, Altynai Asylmuratova and Roberto Bolle, receiving huge ovations. The reception from the press was, as usual, mixed, though the majority liked what Derek had done with the choreography, seeing it as a way of popularising ballet and opening it up to a much wider audience. A significant minority differed, unable to stomach the idea of adapting and changing hallowed choreography in order to make the production genuinely in the round.

The gala performance was a marvellous affair. Princess Diana, then patron of the ENB, arrived looking tanned and radiant and wearing that iconic, pale-blue sequined dress. I was in the line-up to receive her and, because I had seen her during rehearsals, she recognised me and gave me a warm handshake. I sat with my younger daughter, Louise, in the Royal Box.

After the performance, I had to go to the BBC's Television Centre for a confrontation on *Newsnight* with the *Daily Telegraph*'s critic, Ismene Brown, who had written a particularly virulent piece, railing against the dumbing-down of ballet. It was helpful that her colleague on the *Sunday Telegraph* had written a very positive review, which I was able to quote.

Swan Lake has been revived every three or four years ever since and it gives me enormous pride, even though I am no longer directly connected, to see the enduring enthusiasm for this production after so many years.

We had now added arena ballet to the annual calendar at the RAH. Derek Deane's proposal for the following year, Prokofiev's *Romeo and Juliet*, was eagerly accepted by the hall and me. It turned out to be an artistic triumph although a much harder show to sell than *Swan Lake*. Derek filled the arena with jugglers and acrobats as well as an extended corps de ballet. The result was truly spectacular. Derek had promoted Tamara Rojo from within the company and cast her as Juliet. She scored a great personal triumph and it was not surprising when she was snapped up sometime later by the Royal Ballet. *Romeo and Juliet* has been revived from time to time, including one glorious season when Tamara Rojo had returned to ENB as artistic director and was joined by Carlos Acosta for four wonderful performances during the run.

Derek's third in-the-round production at the hall, *Sleeping Beauty*, was less successful, never quite catching the mood of *Swan Lake* and *Romeo and Juliet*. Later on, I myself was instrumental in giving Derek and ENB the idea of setting the music of George Gershwin to dance. The resulting production, *Strictly Gershwin*, proved to be a huge success but was only revived once at the hall after the initial season as ENB considered it outside of their core orbit. A shame, as it could otherwise have been revived many times.

In 2005, Craig Hassall had arrived from Australia to take over the running of ENB. He proved himself an excellent administrator and I was delighted in 2012 when he came to work for my company. By that time, I had almost retired but Craig was a breath of fresh air, breathing new life into every area he touched. I was not at all surprised when he was soon head-hunted by Opera Australia and returned home to Sydney. We kept in close touch and then, suddenly out of the blue, he told me that he was coming over to London the following week for a final interview for the job of CEO at the Royal Albert Hall. He had gone through several rounds on Skype, and now this last one was face-to-face. Whilst we were having lunch the afternoon following his interview, before his imminent departure back home, he took a call to tell him the job was his. Our lunch not surprisingly turned into a very special celebration.

CHAPTER TWENTY-FOUR

PRINCESS DIANA AND THE ROYALS

Without a doubt, the most impressive member of the royal family in terms of giving practical support and encouragement to culture and the arts was the late Princess Diana. As the patron of English National Ballet, she gave her support freely and wholeheartedly. It was very clear that she knew many members within the company individually and had a deep personal interest in both their well-being and success. She really cared in a way which was very unusual for royal patrons who generally floated in and out of events with very little interest if any in what was going on.

Diana's patronage of ENB helped to gain incredible press coverage for the launch of *Swan Lake*. During final preparations at the hall, she was photographed for *The Times* surrounded by all the swans. She was due to leave once the photographer had finished, before the final dress rehearsal got under way. However, she decided she would rather like to stay on and asked if she could. Heather Walker enquired where she would like to sit. 'Oh, up there,' she said, airily pointing to the Royal Box. She stayed there throughout the rehearsal and a news crew from ITV, having been tipped off that she was at the hall, arrived during the second half. Somehow, very much with her encouragement, they managed to get an interview with her sitting in the Royal Box. It ran later that day on the main evening news.

The next day, the Palace contacted the hall. 'Who let her into the Royal Box?' they demanded to know, the Royal Box being owned personally by the monarch. A *faux pas* of magisterial proportion had been committed but it was too late; Princess Diana was a lovely lady who knew exactly what she was doing.

Princess Diana had been at the very first performance of *La Bohème* eighteen months earlier and she told me during the *Swan Lake* rehearsals how much she had enjoyed the production. She was genuinely interested in opera and ballet and the informal atmosphere at the *Swan Lake* rehearsal where she was quite happy to sit back and chat to everyone underlined her commitment to ENB.

With the photo on the front page of *The Times* and the ITV news interview, the remaining tickets soon sold out. It was a promoter's dream to have publicity like this. The *Times* photo has since been reproduced all around the world. English National Ballet had a royal patron who made an enormous difference to their very existence and her death less than two months later was particularly felt by them. Like it or not, no other royal patron has ever enjoyed that amount of influence.

Following the gala night of *Swan Lake*, Princess Diana and others in her party attended a celebratory dinner at the Churchill Hotel. I joined it once I had finished filming for *Newsnight*. I did not quite realise the significance at the dinner of Mr and Mrs Al Fayed, who both seemed on very close terms with the Princess. It was only two months later with the tragic death of Princess Diana and Dodi Al Fayed that the true meaning struck me.

I had first been introduced to Princess Diana at the Royal Academy of Music sometime after I had been made an Honorary Fellow. She had a genuine interest in talking to people with none of the Hanoverian hauteur associated with so many other members of the royal family. Later, I met her again at Wembley, not long before *Turandot*, when I organised a two-day military tattoo for service charities. She came accompanied by eight-year-old Prince Harry who arrived with crayons and paper. These she scooped up at the end of the performance with a knowing smile, fearful no doubt lest they should have ended up in the wrong hands. She was a real beacon that shone on whatever interested her and what she might have been able to do for ENB and so many other arts organisations had she not died so tragically can only be imagined.

I have been privileged to meet the Queen on a number of occasions, including on a visit to the Royal Albert Hall and various receptions at Buckingham Palace, Windsor Castle and the Royal Academy. She always has the most beautiful smile and has done a wonderful job as Queen and Head of State. She will, I fear, be a hard act to follow. She presided over the investiture when I received my CBE back in 2001. I never knew how or why I got the CBE but I think both the Royal Albert Hall and the Royal Philharmonic Orchestra may have had a hand in it.

The first thing I knew was when a letter arrived marked 'From the Prime Minister's Office'. I studied the envelope and wondered who was trying to play tricks on me. Then I opened it and there it was. The PM was minded, it read, to recommend to Her Majesty that I receive the CBE. I was always a bit nonchalant about the honours system but now it was actually me at the receiving end, I suddenly felt rather diffident. Moreover, it was awarded for services to music, a citation which pleased me greatly. I had to keep the news quiet until it was officially announced. Once it had been, I was overwhelmed by the letters I received from friends and colleagues.

When the day for the investiture arrived, I was so delighted that my aunt, my dad's sister and the last of that generation, by then into her nineties, could be present. An ardent monarchist who had lived through the rigours of the war, she was really thrilled to be at Buckingham Palace. As my name was announced and I approached Her Majesty, a uniformed equerry shouted out, 'Music, Ma'am.' 'Oh, you are in music,' said Her Majesty as she placed the honour over my bowed head. As I moved away, an official was all ready to take the award and place it in its case. He must have been well-briefed because when I made some remark about not knowing why I had got it, he said, 'Oh, but you do such wonderful concerts.'

After Diana and the Queen, the other members of the royal family that I have met were rather an anti-climax. Princess Margaret attended the first revival of *Swan Lake* at the Royal Albert Hall. Patrick Deuchar, then still chief executive, asked me if I would like to meet her. When I said I would rather not, he got quite angry and more or less forced me to go up to her with him at the reception following the performance. She was every bit as standoffish and self-centred as I had been led to believe.

Her nephew Prince Andrew took over the royal patronage of ENB and attended a couple of performances at the RAH over the years, including one where the great Alicia Markova was also a guest in the Royal Box. He pretty well ignored her all evening, was clearly bored stiff by the performance and only became animated when he picked up that one of the male dancers had worked his way through half of the young ladies in the corps de ballet.

I once attended a wonderful dinner and reception at Buckingham Palace in celebration of Yehudi Menuhin who conducted his School Orchestra in the Music Room. The Queen Mother was still alive and sat immediately in front of John and Norma Major, who displayed an exaggerated bow and curtsy whenever she got up. She in turn kept looking round at them with a stern, unsmiling glare. I can only speculate on the reason. Yehudi was in his element and spoke to the assembled royals and others. In his speech, he was insistent on running through all of the royals present including royal families which had long since disappeared but were still clearly recognised within Buckingham Palace. Thus we had tributes to the royal houses of Romania, Yugoslavia, Greece, Italy and Bulgaria. It was a wonderful if bizarre evening and a welcome feeling of normality returned to me as I exited the palace gates.

CHAPTER TWENTY-FIVE

THE THREE TENORS

Once people know that I work in the music business, the question I get frequently asked is whether I have worked with the three tenors. I have been able to reply that, yes, I have, although not with them all together, and not always with them singing. Pavarotti was the first and it happened in 1984 when his London manager, John Coast, called to ask whether I could arrange a masterclass for Pavarotti. This was in the era before Withholding Tax was introduced and, under the old tax regime, Pavarotti needed to protect his tax status in the UK by taking a paid engagement before his tax year ended. John Coast told me that he was free on a certain date in between travelling from the USA to Italy but that he would be too tired to sing and hence the idea of the masterclass.

The Barbican happened to have the date available and so we set about making detailed arrangements. John suggested four young singers to take part in the first part of the programme, whilst in the second half, the audience would have the opportunity to ask questions. It seemed this would make the basis for an interesting evening and I kept the seat prices reasonable, bearing in mind that Pavarotti would not be singing. John asked me to provide a dozen or so different types of seats so that Pavarotti could choose one that suited him. We hired in a variety of thrones and elegant chairs, all of them on the largish size. So the first thing Pavarotti saw when he arrived in the middle of the afternoon was our wonderful selection of seats. He laughed uproariously and produced from his shoulder bag a small, chromium-plated circular stool in two parts which he screwed together — that, he announced, was what he would use.

Before we could finalise his technical arrangements, John Coast told me that Pavarotti was going to listen to a young British tenor. We all sat back in the auditorium, expecting to hear some new discovery, imagining that anyone who had got through the tiers of management surrounding Pavarotti and who was actually going to sing to him must be really something. Well, I was wrong, very wrong. The strangulated tones of the young hopeful showed that here was a lad, untrained and without a lot of natural talent, but with a very pushy mother in attendance, who had somehow managed to persuade the world's leading tenor to spare time to listen to him. My admiration for Pavarotti leapt several notches when I heard him take a great deal of time and trouble giving good, sound advice to the young man and his mother. They were let down very gently and went away looking quite happy. Yet Pavarotti had been honest with them and had told them nothing but the truth.

Only when the audition was finished could we begin the rehearsal, or rather, the walk through, mainly for the benefit of the BBC camera crew who were recording the evening. They nearly did not get to cover the show. With its usual arrogance, the BBC had, without reference to me, tied up Pavarotti and the singers and offered me a derisory facility fee, which I promptly turned down. All their arguments about not being able to record the evening if we did not play ball were in vain. I told them I really did not care whether it was recorded or not and, little by little, the fee offer increased until at last it reached a figure I was happy with.

The first half of the evening went very well with the four singers being put through their paces by the maestro. The performance by Kim Begley, a wonderful operatic tenor, understandably came in for the most detailed analysis but all four singers felt they had benefited hugely from Pavarotti's comments. In the second half, Pavarotti answered questions posed by members of the audience. It turned out to be a charming, informal session with Pavarotti in a relaxed mood displaying a lovely self-deprecating sense of humour. When somebody asked him about his film debut in *Hey, Giorgio* and the rather lukewarm response he had received from the press, he cheerfully replied with total honesty that he thought he had not been very good.

Afterwards, we had a reception for him in the Garden Room at the Barbican. I could see that Henry Wrong, the centre's director, was feeling really chuffed that I had actually managed to get Pavarotti to the Barbican, even in a non-singing capacity, as Henry had been convinced that he was not going to show up. Pavarotti and his lady secretary stayed for nearly an hour and, as they were about to leave, one of the guests who had just been served the dessert at the buffet ran across to shake Pavarotti by the hand as he headed for the door. Pavarotti graciously took his hand but with his free hand he could not resist scooping up the poor man's dessert — it was apple crumble and cream. I have a lasting image of the great tenor smiling and waving as he left whilst licking off the remains of the crumble and cream on his other hand.

Jose Carreras, unlike Pavarotti, did sing in the few concerts when I worked with him. He was under contract to IMG, Mark McCormack's sports and entertainment conglomerate. They were keen to try Carreras in arenas and wanted a risk partner. I think they came to me as it was during the time when I had a very strong tie-up with the *Daily Telegraph*, which enabled me to place enormous advertisements in the paper. Although, having said that, sometimes these actually appeared as planned although as they were free they were quite often pulled at the last minute in favour of something more immediately profitable.

The first concert at the NEC in Birmingham was enormous fun. Carreras was on a fixed if very substantial fee and so with eight thousand people in attendance it was possible to make a profit. The next concert in Manchester some months later was less so. Carreras was now on a guarantee plus a share of the profit and it was no longer so easy to make any real money given the high risk involved. IMG had an international contract with Carreras and so we found that they would give in to almost any demand, whatever the financial consequences for IMG and me, in order to keep their artist happy. It was an alien way of working for me and I decided that, as much as I enjoyed the fun of working on this scale, it was not a very profitable line down which to continue. It was also clear that Carreras was not an arena artist as he did not have the pulling power to sustain the ten thousand or more people needed to fill such venues. Even his physical presence was much more suited to more conventional venues.

We did one last date with Carreras at the Royal Albert Hall, which proved a much more congenial atmosphere for him. It was made memorable by my good friend Ian Maclay, who was then managing the BBC Concert Orchestra, which was playing for the concert. Looking at his watch after yet another encore, he said very loudly, 'Oh no, Ray, not another bleeding encore. How many more is he going to do, for God's sake?' Fritz, Carreras's valet and general factotum was standing nearby. With his thick Austrian accent, he asked, 'Who is this man?' In another era, Ian might have found himself being marched off to somewhere rather sinister.

Placido Domingo came my way via the Philharmonia Orchestra which had toured with him as their conductor. They now told me that he would like to do the same programme in London so I booked the Royal Festival Hall for a Saturday night and was surprised to find how slowly it sold. In the end, we got to nearly a full house. It was a pleasant evening but rather bizarre. I felt the two and a half thousand people were there to see someone who they would rather see looking at them with his mouth open and all they got was a picture of his backside.

The nearest I got to actually presenting the Three Tenors was when I was presenting *Turandot* at Wembley and I put an advertisement in the *Evening Standard* headed: 'You don't need three tenners to come to *Turandot* – you can get in for two fivers.'

CHAPTER TWENTY-SIX

ALMOST AN IMPRESARIO

The opportunity for me to sell the company I had started, developed and nurtured for well over forty years came out of the blue from a rather unexpected quarter.

In 2005, a German entertainment group promoted a tour of *Classical Spectacular* in Germany. I was not impressed by their management skills and even less so when the managing director told me, during somebody else's rather tawdry mega-production of Verdi's opera *Nabucco* at the Stade de France in Paris, that 'opera is so boring'. But I was at least glad that Berlin was included in the schedule – the city where my mother had resided during the 1920s and for which she had always had enormous affection. One day, I was walking backstage immediately after the end of a performance of *Classical Spectacular* at the Velodrome, which had finished with Tchaikovsky's 1812 *Overture* complete with cannon effects and pyrotechnics. The smell of cordite was hanging in the air as we passed an elderly couple heading for the exit. My German, though far from good, was sufficient for me to understand the lady saying, 'Hans, do you remember that smell? Just like the war.'

Later, on the same tour, I found time to visit Leipzig, of which my mother had often spoken, and also Dresden. The Frauenkirche there had only recently been fully restored. It was a salutary moment to enter the church in all its magnificent rococo glory and to reflect for some moments. That this was also the country of Beethoven, Bach, Schiller and Goethe and many more besides brought home to me once again that we can forgive but we must never forget. Despite our faith in democracy, the potential for despots to take power and alter the lives of the many will never go away.

.....
211

When I got back to London, the company called. The managing director would like to chat to me when he came to London. We met up and he came quickly to the point, did I want to sell the business? Later I flew to Berlin for the day to continue talking. He showed me over his house in one of the more affluent suburbs with its gym downstairs in the basement. During the tour, he mentioned his previous house, which apparently had a swimming pool as well as a gym. Using an appropriate Anglo-Saxon expletive he boasted to me of how many ladies he had entertained there. It reminded me of Leporello in Mozart's *Don Giovanni*, listing his master's conquests.

So why did I sell to him? The truth is that the offer was a good one; it was as simple as that. I felt also that the dependence I had on the Royal Albert Hall was perhaps too great and might not last for ever, particularly if they put more focus on promoting their own shows, something that seemed to be in the air. In any case, I felt I had done my bit. I firmly believed in the 'promoter's nose' – the ability to sniff whether the germ of an idea would work, what artists to work with, how to set the seat prices. And this very same promoter's nose was telling me that it was time to stand aside and let someone else have a go. I had started to find that I had less hunger for rooting out new business, an essential part of the trade.

My family, which now included six grandchildren, was so important to me and when my elder brother died I also felt increasing responsibility for his seven young grandchildren. I had had a very full-on workload for decades – the hours involved in being a promoter had cost me my marriage and curtailed my social life. After all, most performances are in the evenings and at weekends when others are at their leisure. Christmas was a time of intensive hard work with concerts around the country as well as a heavy concentration in London. I knew it was time to sell up and that is what the German offer enabled me to do.

'Every dog has its day,' as the saying goes and I knew I had enjoyed the glory days at the Royal Albert Hall. I was only too aware how public tastes change and every generation has its young Turks who emerge to challenge the more established promoters and producers. I myself had occupied that position when I emerged from touring small concerts around the country to engage in larger scale concerts and events. I was thirty-six when the Barbican opened in 1982, giving me a fantastic opportunity to develop and enlarge my presence particularly in London but also in the regions.

When I returned to the Royal Albert Hall with *Classical Spectacular* in 1989, it was in hindsight an opportune moment to re-engage with the hall at a time when its fortunes were running at a low ebb. The arrival of Patrick Deuchar soon afterwards marked the start of its rapid ascent towards what it has become today. I was very glad to work with him on developing the operas and the ballet productions and much else. At one time, I was presenting close to one hundred performances a year there. I would not have liked to be hanging on as the number declined steadily owing to the hall's development as a producer in its own right. Prescient thoughts indeed in view of what has happened there after I sold up. As in the event I was right – the hall took over the Christmas Festival slot themselves and also worked directly with English National Ballet. Dare I say that I had shown them a few tricks over the years and now they no longer had need of any outside help to mount these shows. The opera productions also drew to a close after the takeover of my company through lack of investment in new productions with bolder and inevitably more expensive artistic values, which I had suggested. I do take pride from the comments made to me by the RAH's management team after I left, that had I remained actively in charge of my old company they would not have acted as they did, but who really knows?

When I look back over the decades that I worked as a promoter, I can see the changing face of Britain reflected in the shows that I put on. When I started, the arrival of a Gilbert and Sullivan concert at the Civic Theatre, Rotherham, or the Theatre Royal, St Helens, or at any number of smaller venues, was eagerly awaited by local audiences who had snapped up most if not all of the tickets. This was still the time when pre-war musicals like *The Student Prince* and *The Desert Song* were touring alongside hit Broadway shows from the 1940s and 1950s. There were still a few gritty black-and-white movies being produced; not everything was yet in colour. Television was also exclusively black and white until the advent of colour in 1971.

I was a child of my time, moving on with changing tastes as one era flowed into the next. Anthony Eden had played the last card of gunboat diplomacy with the Suez fiasco in 1956. The Empire and colonies as we had known them were largely gone by the mid-1960s. Imperial glory had given way to a more modest role for the nation. In my own world, Harold Wilson's victory in 1964 heralded a much greater appreciation of the arts and I was there to take advantage of this more enlightened era. I had been born amongst 'Joe Public' — it was the audience that influenced musical tastes. My mum and dad were very much of that era. In our case, music ran in the family and with me it just happened to show itself not in performing but in programming and producing. Of course I learnt from my peers, from listening to what people told me and by trying to satisfy the demand. In the end though, it came down to my making the correct decisions about what to put on and fortunately I mostly got it right. Though, of course, not always ...

I have always been pleasantly surprised by the feedback I have been given over the years with many people telling me that the first concert they ever attended as youngsters was one of mine. I have even seen the odd familiar face in the audience, such as when Frankie Howerd came with his sister and her family to the Opera Gala Night — my first concert back in 1982 at the newly opened Barbican. Much more recently, I was delighted to hear that Inspector Morse himself, John Thaw, and his wife Sheila Hancock used to discreetly attend many of my concerts over the years. I was never aware of that at the time but the thought of 'Morse' himself coming to listen to some of the music he loved so much is very touching.

In the years just before I sold the company and in the period immediately afterwards when I continued to run it for a short time, I presented many very big artists — Anna Netrebko, Jonas Kaufman, Bryn Terfel amongst them — as well as co-promoting seasons by the American Ballet Theatre, Carlos Acosta, and New York City Ballet. It was always exciting to work with such great artists but nothing for me can replace the thrill of creating something by oneself.

Programming a whole range of symphony and other concerts at the fledgling Barbican was so exciting. The Royal Albert Hall has also been a really very special part of my life; whenever I went there, whether for a rehearsal or a performance, the atmosphere was always something exhilarating and so creating shows specially for the hall was always an enormous and challenging pleasure. Yet above all, it was those early days, when I set out with three or four singers and a pianist with our simple but popular programmes, that still make me glow — they really were the most marvellous of times. Though why anyone would have had faith in a twenty-year-old lad touting concert proposals around the country is beyond me. That professional singers had confidence in a young whippersnapper with no track record still astounds me. And yet the confidence and loyalty that they all gave me allowed me to build a business and a brand. I really have been very lucky to do throughout my working life the things that have given me so much pleasure. The critics may sometimes have carped but the public always remained very loyal. As I enjoy my retirement with grandchildren, travelling and much more besides, I thank them all for nearly sixty years of support. Without an audience, I would never have had a business.

The world in 2021 is a much more challenging place and nobody is quite sure whether in the end all the pieces will go back together again exactly as they were. I am quietly confident that no amount of state-of-the-art digital performances will ever replace being there, at a live event. The performing arts have survived through thick and thin and will emerge in whatever form ready to please, entertain and enlighten audiences for a long time to come. I'm only grateful I was given a chance to be a part of this wonderful world.

I can leave the final words, as I did the opening three questions at the start of this book, to Victor Hochhauser, who said after the Barbican opened:

'Raymond Gubbay, Raymond Gubbay, he's doing so many concerts nowadays, you could almost call him an impresario.'

INDEX